The Selected Levis

PITT POETRY SERIES

ED OCHESTER, EDITOR

The Selected Levis

REVISED EDITION

LARRY LEVIS

Selected and with an afterword by David St. John

University of Pittsburgh Press

The publication of this book is supported by a grant from the
Pennsylvania Council on the Arts

ISBN 0-8229-5793-0

Contents

WINTER STARS

THE WIDENING SPELL OF THE LEAVES

ELEGY

Wrecking Crew

My poem would eat nothing.
I tried giving it water
but it said no,

worrying me.
Day after day,
I held it up to the light,

turning it over,
but it only pressed its lips
more tightly together.

It grew sullen, like a toad
through with being teased.
I offered it all my money,

my clothes, my car with a full tank.
But the poem stared at the floor.
Finally I cupped it in

my hands, and carried it gently
out into the soft air, into the
evening traffic, wondering how

to end things between us.
For now it had begun breathing,
putting on more and

more hard rings of flesh.
And the poem demanded the food,
it drank up all the water,

beat me and took my money,
tore the faded clothes
off my back,

said Shit,
and walked slowly away,
slicking its hair down.

Said it was going
over to your place.

✌ Magician Poems

1. The Magician's Exit Wound

All day
the sky has the look of dirty paper.
My shadow stays indoors.
I watch its step,

and plan my tricks.
This evening,
the loneliness of disappearing acts!
I think of

poking my head through the sky,
and, in those frozen pressures,
of breaking into
blood on a cloud.

2. The Magician's Ride to the Hospital

Just now
I noticed my arms,
how they act without even telling me anymore,
their preference for rain and razor blades,

or for simply dropping off,
like forgotten two-by-fours falling off
half built houses.
Now they grab at me like stubborn interns.

                              I turn quickly, mirrored
in the dark glass of the ambulance,
where already
my face is wood, and painted to a doll's
astonished whites and reds.

Outside even the sky is shocked and darkens.

3. The Magician's Face

One day all the smiles hardened;
pals frowned like a firing squad and closed in.
So I got lost in
cafeterias,

in the waiting rooms of airports,
and tapped my fingers,
until I was
alone as a paper scrap under someone's heel.

Then a funny thing happened.
I did a real trick—
sitting still while a plane roared off,
I made a face like

a single window smashed and bare with sky.

4. The Magician at His Own Revival

Once I thought my mouth was a scar
that disappeared
like spittle being wiped off of a plate.
So I shut up

and sulked
like last year's inner tube that hangs
in a noose all winter
through the rain.

I sat through the chatter.
Then somebody bared his teeth and jeered.
I rose. I called out
like a blind man drifting on the drifting ice,

for no reason at all but me, me.

5. The Magician's Call

Our conversation
frays like an old wire in the rain—
its thinness crackles.
And there's a silence as the phone's hung up,

as frank as someone's heels walking out.
Outside in lightning,
the palm trees whiten quickly and go bald
as the fronds crack

in the wind.
"Eat shit," says someone pushing me away;
and my father's
vanished with a smell of fear and forever

just under his breath in the static.

6. The Magician's Edge and Exit

I've got my edge now—
as a lone end of a sheet quivers on the line
and waits for the
flick of someone's nail in the wind,

and a lost
pocketknife rusts on the railings,
where the fence boards warp and blister.
Now driving I whip

the wheel back and forth—
as a frayed tire skids on the ice,
and a back fence looms like flesh turned inside out
in the noise.

And I drift through it, suddenly air.

7. The Magician Ending

After a while my lungs give
like shale keeling off without a sound.
And I don't hear anything as I let the flesh go,
and open out

like a diver,
my arms spreading beyond their own nerves,
as a shrug of stars and years
drifts through me.

1. Convalescent Home

High on painkillers,
the old don't hear
their bones hollering
anything tonight.
   They turn
harmless and furry, licking
themselves good-bye

They are the small animals vanishing
at the road's edge everywhere

2. The Myth

The go-go girl yawns.
The cheap dye
her mother swiped from
a five-and-ten has turned
her hair green,
but her eyes are flat
and still as thumbprints, or
the dead presidents pressed
into coins.
     She glints
    She is like
the screen flickering in
an empty movie house
far into the night.

3. Spider

In the bruised doorway
that has been jimmied open,
even the dark spider shines,
tears at its belly
and moves sideways a little
on its web, swaying,

while my hand on this pencil
knows nothing,
moves back and
forth, takes hold
of things, is never sorry

For Stones

Against laws
the tongue tries to go back down the throat
it gets uncontrollable   it lies

while flickering everywhere are
knuckles, teeth, fists nobody saw, hair
drifting from wires,
eyes that stopped closing heavily and met
the ax and the train head on—
all the die-hards
who kept the faith with the stones

stones that will open at a touch, breathe
and spread like water like

plain water that is simple and against the law

Fish

for Philip Levine

The cop holds me up like a fish;
he feels the huge bones
surrounding my eyes,
and he runs a thumb under them,

lifting my eyelids
as if they were
envelopes filled with the night.
Now he turns

my head back and forth, gently,
until I'm so tame and still
I could be a tiny, plastic
skull left on the

dashboard of a junked car.
By now he's so sure of me
he chews gum,
and drops his flashlight to his side;

he could be cleaning a trout
while the pines rise into the darkness,
though tonight trout
are freezing into bits of stars

under the ice. When he lets me go
I feel numb. I feel like
a fish burned by his touch, and turn
and slip into the cold

night rippling with neons,
and the razor blades
of the poor,
and the torn mouths on posters.

Once, I thought even through this
I could go quietly as a star
turning over and over
in the deep truce of its light.

Now, I must
go on repeating the last, filthy
words on the lips
of this shrunken head,

shining out of its death in the moon—
until trout surface
with their petrified, round eyes,
and the stars begin moving.

For the Country

1.

One of them undid your blouse, then
used a pocketknife to
cut away your skirt
like he'd take
fur off some limp thing,
or slice up the belly of a fish.

Pools of rainwater shone in the sunlight,
and they took turns.

2.

After it was over,
you stared up, maybe,
at the blue sky where the shingles were missing,
the only sounds
pigeons
walking the rafters, their eyes fixed, shining,
the sound of water dripping.
The idiot drool of the cattle. Flies.

3.

You are the sweet, pregnant,
teen-age blonde thrown from the speeding car.

You are a dead, clean-shaven astronaut
orbiting perfectly forever.

You are America.
You are nobody.
I made you up.
I take pills and drive a flammable truck
until I drop.

I am the nicest guy in the world,
closing his switchblade and whistling.

4.

The plum blossoms have
been driven into a silence all
their own,
as I go on
driving an old red tractor
with a busted seat.
The teeth of its gears
chatter in a faint language
of mad farmwives who have whittled,
and sung tunelessly,
over the dog turds in their front yards,
for the last hundred years.

5.

And I will say nothing, anymore, of
my country,
nor of my wife reading about abortions,
nor of the birds that
have circled high over my
head, following me,
for days.

I will close my eyes,
and grit my teeth,
and slump down further in
my chair,
and watch what goes on
behind my eyelids:
stare at the dead horses with flowers stuck in
their mouths—

and that is the end of it.

This moon a pig spits out on a hot night.
So empty, it spins when no one
thinks of it, looks it in the face.
You can pin it down with your eye,
your little eye. Make it stop.
Let it go.

The town I grew up in
has a drug store where men
gather, since their words
fall into the tiny graves
rain makes in their tracks.
So it goes.

In the town of 20 pool cues,
of noses broken over the feel of pussy,
among the bottles of grease and candy
lining the shelves,
the men laughed,
they stole cars and left them in ditches, smoldering.
Their wives, spitting at irons, never looked up.
They grew older.

Hair slicked back in jail,
their eyes studied everything.
Big snakes pulled out of holes,
they weaned themselves, they grew quieter,
they multiplied.

When one of them died it took a day.
He did it the way
a snail curls up into its shell
and disappears. He left only a flat
spot on the earth. On a hot day.

And I drive slowly up and down the streets,
radio blaring, under
the moon's sweating thumb.

Maybe the Dead

Maybe the dead know the ant's troubles,
or the debts snails pay out with their bodies
until only the shells remain glistening,
or the sweet tooth under the worm's lip.

As a child asleep, I dreamt
the Sierras drifting out of my right side,
the Pacific coming in on my left,

until mountains became unimportant.
The sea, too, went away,

and I was beaten hard in the face with a board
in a men's room in Modesto,
and felt around, buglike, with a terrific silence—
watching a pigeon settle on a roof, and
clean itself under one wing with its beak

Here are all the shadows that have fallen on
no one in particular
Here is the water coming in under the pier
Here is the untouchable woman who sticks out her tongue
Here is the ax handle driven into the pig's snout
Here are the separated legs of an ant, pulled off one
by one out of boredom
and the stack of dried fish left as an offering
to the bulldozer ticking in the sunlight
Here is the fist of the president falling onto what he imagines
is a table full of multicolored lizards
And here is a multicolored lizard quickly fading into grass
leaving his strange tattoo in the colors of your eyes
I walk the cut road for miles
where the ground is freezing in the name of the father,
and the ghost of the cracked snout, and the dull sons
wielding ax handles in the slaughterhouse Day of Our Lord
ruled by bellies. Ruled by the longings of toys
left under houses for years. Left as offerings. Dust.
Puzzles for the woman turned to a doorstep. Over which
you carried all the dead at the moment of your birth

The Afterlife

Rhododendrons

Winter has moved off
somewhere, writing its journals
in ice.

But I am still afraid to move,
afraid to speak,
as if I lived in a house
wallpapered with the cries of birds
I cannot identify.

Beneath the trees
a young couple sits talking
about the afterlife,
where no one, I think, is
whittling toys for the stillborn.
I laugh,

but I don't know.
Maybe the whole world is absentminded
or floating. Maybe the new lovers undress
without wondering how
the snow grows over the Andes,
or how a horse cannot remember those
frozen in the sleigh behind it,
but keeps running until the lines tangle,
while the dead sit coolly beneath their pet stars.

As I write this,
some blown rhododendrons are nodding
in the first breezes. I want
to resemble them, and remember nothing,
the way a photograph of an excavation
cannot remember the sun.

The wind rises or stops
and it means nothing.

I want to be circular;
a pond or a column of smoke
revolving, slowly, its ashes.

I want to turn back and go up
to myself at age 20,
and press five dollars into his hand
so he can sleep.
While he stands trembling on a street in Fresno,
suddenly one among many in the crowd
that strolls down Fulton Street,
among the stores that are closing,
and is never heard of again.

Out here, I can say anything.
I can say, for example, that a girl
disappearing tonight
will sleep or stare out
fixedly as the train moves her
into its adulthood of dust
and sidings.

I remember watching wasps
on hot evenings
fly heavily over chandeliers
in hotel lobbies.
They've torn them down, too.
And the elderly drunks
who seemed not to mind anything,
who seemed to look for change
in their pockets, as they gazed
at the girl in the Pepsi ad,
and the girl who posed for the ad,
must all be dead now.

I can aleady tell that this
is no poem to show you,
this love poem. It's so
flat spoken and ignorable,
like the man chain smoking
who discovers he's
no longer waiting for anyone,
and goes to the movies
alone each Saturday, and grins,
and likes them.
This poem so like the hour
when the street lights turn

amber and blink, and the calm
professor burns another book,
and the divorcee waters her one
chronically dying plant.
This poem so like me
it could be my double.

I have stood for a long time
in its shadow, the way I stood
in the shadow of a dead roommate
I had to cut down from the ceiling
on Easter break, when
I was young.

That night I put my car
in neutral, and cut the engine
and lights to glide downhill
and hear the wind rush over
the dead metal.
I had to know what it felt
like, and under the moon,
gaining speed, I wanted to slip
out of my body and be
done with it.

A man can give up smoking
and the movies, and live for years
hearing the wind tick over roofs
but never looking up from
his one page, or the tiny
life he keeps carving over and
over upon it. And when everyone
around him dies, he can move
a grand piano into
his house, and sit down
alone, and finally play,

certain that no one will
overhear him, though he plays
as loud as he can,
so that when the dead come
and take his hands off the keys
they are invisible, the way air
and music are not.

Signs

1.

All night I dreamed of my home,
of the roads that are so long
and straight they die in the middle—
among the spines of elderly weeds
on either side, among the dead cats,
the ants who are all eyes, the suitcase
thrown open, sprouting failures.

2.

And this evening in the garden
I find the winter
inside a snail shell, rigid and
cool, a little stubborn temple,
its one visitor gone.

3.

If there were messages or signs,
I might hear now a voice tell me
to walk forever, to ask
the mold for pardon, and one
by one I would hear out my sins,
hear they are not important—that I am
part of this rain
drumming its long fingers, and
of the roadside stone refusing
to blink, and of the coyote
nailed to the fence with its
long grin.

And when there are no messages
the dead lie still—
their hands crossed so strangely
like knives and forks after supper.

4.

I stay up late listening.
My feet tap the floor,
they begin a tiny dance
which will outlive me.
They turn away from this poem.
It is almost Spring.

You sail placidly down the Orinoco in a white dress.
You cross your legs and accept a drink from a stranger.
But then your mother and father, dragging the dead mule
Out of the shade, begin waving and calling.

You can swim over and kneel beside the animal.
Speaking softly, you do not disturb the toucan,
Who dreams, on the branch just above you,
That his stripes have grown younger.

Your mother and father kneel behind you
And flutter their hands weakly as if in prayer, until
It seems you too are clutching a limb with huge claws,
As the skin over each knuckle hardens.

You grip deeply, until there is no future but this.
You think of your rented house trailer,
Of the smoke that is rising bashfully
Out of all the chimneys at once in Boise, Idaho.

But you suspect something.
The jungle is too green.
The mule's lips are becoming a little too intimate.
And these two aren't your real parents.

for M.

1.

Looking into the eyes of Gerard de Nerval
You notice the giant sea crabs rising.
Which is what happens
When you look into the eyes of Gerard de Nerval,
Always the same thing: the giant sea crabs,
The claws in their vague red holsters
Moving around, a little doubtfully.

2.

But looking into the eyes of Pierre Reverdy
Is like throwing the editorial page
Out into the rain
And then riding alone on the subway.

Also, it is like avoiding your father.
You are hiding and he looks for you
Under each vine; he is coming nearer
And nearer. What can you do
But ignore him?

3.

In either case, soon you are riding alone on a subway.
Which is not important.
What is important is to avoid
Looking too closely into the eyes of your father,
That formal eclipse.

Your friends nod. Their glances are like huts
In which tools have been abandoned.
Maybe you have already begun dying.
Someone bumps into you and it takes root,
A low shrub, disinterested.

So you work late in an office building
While a man vacuums the floors.

You go further into the blank paper.
You go past the white smirk of the benign.
You find the dark trousers of your father,
The hairpins of your mother.
You hold them in your hands,

While the jails are closing in Santiago
And the sores on the gelding's withers
Are ordinary. They glisten in the rain
Outside the jail, and say nothing.

It was 1946 and the war was over.
Your father hung his trousers on the bed.
Your mother undressed and shook out her hair.
They moved closer. As you began,
They blindfolded the horse and led him further
Up the cliff while the shadows
Pulled on their gloves one by one and went out,
And left them alone.

The Crimes of the Shade Trees

Today everyone forgave me.
No one mentioned the felony
Of my back against the oak,
Or the air I was breathing, earlier.
So it is possible I am not Levis.

I smoke and I think possibly
I am the smoke—
Drifting through Omaha as smoke does,
Past the new sofas on sale.
Past the south view of the slaughterhouse,
And the shade trees flushing with light.

And it doesn't matter.
For example, if I am really
Something ordinary, a doorstep,
Or the gleaming of frost on someone's lawn
As he shaves, that would be all right.

I only mention this
To the caretaker of my absence,
Who dozes on a beige sofa.

While she knits us a bible
In which the blind remain blind,
Like shade trees. Filling with light,

Each leaf feels its way out,
Each a mad bible of patience.

Linnets

1.

One morning with a 12-gauge my brother shot
what he said was a linnet. He did this at close range
where it sang on a flowering almond branch. Any-
one could have done the same and shrugged it off,
but my brother joked about it for days, describing
how nothing remained of it, how he watched for
feathers and counted only two gold ones which he
slipped behind his ear. He grew uneasy and care-
less; nothing remained. He wore loud ties and two
tone shoes. He sold shoes, he sold soap. Nothing
remained. He drove on the roads with a little hole
in the air behind him.

2.

But in the high court of linnets he does not get
off so easily. He is judged and sentenced to pull me
on a rough cart through town. He is further pun-
ished since each feather of the dead bird falls around
me, not him, and each falls as a separate linnet, and
each feather lost from one of these becomes a lin-
net. While he is condemned to feel nothing ever
settle on his shoulders, which are hunched over and
still, linnets gather around me. In their singing,
they cleanse my ears of all language but that of
linnets. My gaze takes on the terrible gaze of song
birds. And I find that I too am condemned, and
must stitch together, out of glue, loose feathers,
droppings, weeds and garbage I find along the
street, the original linnet, or, if I fail, be condemned
to be pulled in a cart by my brother forever. We
are tired of each other, tired of being brothers like
this. The backside of his head, close cropped, is what
I notice when I look up from work. To fashion

the eyes, the gaze, the tongue and trance of a linnet
is impossible. The eyelids are impossibly delicate
and thin. I am dragged through the striped zoo of
the town. One day I throw down the first stillborn
linnet, then another, then more. Then one of them
begins singing.

3.

As my brother walks through an intersection the
noise from hundreds of thin wings, linnet wings,
becomes his silence. He shouts in his loud clothes
all day. God grows balder.

4.

Whales dry up on beaches by themselves.
The large bones in their heads, their silence,
is a way of turning inward.

Elephants die in exile.
Their tusks begin curling, begin growing
into their skulls.

My father once stopped a stray dog
with a 12-gauge, a blast in the spine.
But you see them on the roads, trotting through the rain.

Cattle are slaughtered routinely.
But pigs are intelligent and vicious to the end.
Their squeals burn circles.

Mice are running over the freezing snow.
Wolverines will destroy kitchens for pleasure.
Wolverines are so terrible you must give in.

The waist of a weasel is also lovely. It slips away.

The skies under the turtle's shell are birdless.

These shadows become carp rising slowly. The black
trees are green again. The creeks are full
and the wooden bridge trembles.

The suicides slip beneath you, shining.
You think if you watched them long enough
you would become fluent in their ten foreign tongues

of light and drummed fingers and inbreedings.

5.

Snakes swallow birds, mice, anything warm.
Beaten to death with a length of pipe,
a snake will move for hours afterward, digesting.

In fact their death takes too long.
In their stillness it may be they outlast death.
They are like stones the moment after

a wind passes over.
The tough skin around a snake's eyes
is ignorant and eternal.

They are made into belts and wallets.
Their delicate meat can be eaten.
But you can't be sure.

In the morning another snake lies curled
on the branch just over your head.

Under the saint's heel in the painting,
a gopher snake sleeps.
The saint's eyes are syphilitic with vision.

He looks the Lord in the face.
He is like the bridge the laborers shrug at
as they wade across the water at night.

When LaBonna Stivers brought a 4 foot bullsnake
to High Mass, she stroked its lifted throat;
she smiled: 'Snakes don't have no minds.'

6.

You can't be sure. Your whole family
may be wiped out by cholera. As the plums
blossom, you may hang yourself.

Or you may love a woman whose low laugh
makes her belly shake softly.
She wants you to stay, and you should have.

Or like your brother, you may go
into the almond orchard to kill
whatever moves. You may want to go

against the little psalms and clear gazings
of birds, against yourself, a 12-gauge
crooked negligently over your shoulder.

You're tired of summer.
You want to stop all the singing.
And everything is singing.

At close range you blow a linnet
into nothing at all, into the silence
of stumps, where everyone sits and whittles.

Your brother grows into a stranger.
He walks into town in the rain.
Two gold feathers behind his ear.

He is too indifferent to wave.
He buys all the rain ahead of him,
and sells all the silence behind him.

7. Linnet Taxidermy

I thought when finished
it would break into flight, its beak
a Chinese trumpet over the deepest lakes.
But with each feather it grows colder to the touch.
I attach wings which wait for the glacier
to slide under them. The viewpoint of ice
is birdless. I close my eyes,
I give up.

I meet my brother in Los Angeles.
I offer him rain
but he clears his throat.
He offers me
the freeway and the sullen huts;
the ring fingers stiffening;
the bitten words.

There are no birds he remembers.
He does not remember owning a gun.
He remembers nothing of the past.

He is whistling 'Kansas City'
on Hollywood Boulevard, a bird
with half its skull eaten away
in the shoebox tucked under his arm.

When the matinee ends, the lights come on
and we blink slowly
and we walk out. It is the hour
when the bald usher
falls in love.

When we are the night and the rain,
the leper on his crutch will spit once,
and go on singing.

8. Matinee

Your family stands over your bed
like Auks of estrangement.
You ask them to look you in the eye,
in the flaming aviary.
But they float over in dirigibles:

in one of them
a girl is undressing; in another
you are waking your father.

Your wife lies hurt on the roadside
and you must find her.
You drive slowly, looking.

They lift higher and higher
over the snow on the Great Plains.
Goodbye, tender blimps.

9. 1973

At the end of winter
the hogs are eating abandoned cars.
We must choose between Jesus and seconal
as we walk under the big, casual spiders whitening
in ice, in tree tops. These great elms rooted in hell
hum so calmly.

My brother marching through Prussia
wears a chrome tie and sings.
Girls smoothing their dresses
become mothers. Trees grow more deeply
into the still farms.

The war ends.
A widow cradles her husband's
acetylene torch,
the flame turns blue,
a sparrow flies out of the bare elm
and it begins again.

I'm no one's father.
I whittle a linnet out of wood until
the bus goes completely dark around me.
The farms in their white patients' smocks join hands.
Only the blind can smell water,
the streams moving a little,
freezing and thawing.

In Illinois one bridge is made entirely
of dead linnets. When the river sings under them,
their ruffled feathers turn large and black.

10. At the High Meadow

It's March; the arthritic horses
stand in the same place
all day.
A piebald mare flicks her ears back.

Ants have already taken over
the eyes of the house finch
on the sill.

So you think someone
is coming,
someone already passing the burned mill,
someone with news of a city
built on snow.

But over the bare table
in the morning
a glass of water goes blind
from staring upward.

For you
it's not so easy.
You begin the long witnessing:
Table. Glass of water. Lone crow
circling.

You witness the rain for weeks
and there are only two of you.
You divide yourself in two and witness yourself,
and it makes no difference.

You think of God dying of anthrax
in a little shed, of a matinee
in which three people sit
with their hands folded and a fourth
coughs. You come down the mountain.

11.

Until one day in a diner in Oakland
you begin dying.
It is peace time.
You have no brother.
You never had a brother.
In the matinees no one sat next to you.
This brother for whom
you have been repairing linnets all your life,
unthankful stuffed little corpses,
hoping they'd perch behind glass in museums
that have been leveled, this brother
who slept under the fig tree
turning its dark glove inside out at noon, is no one;
the strong back you rode while
the quail sang perfect triangles, was no one's.
Your shy father extinct in a single footprint,
your mother a stone growing a cuticle.
It is being suggested that you were never born, that
it never happened in linnet feathers
clinging to the storm fence along the freeway;
in the Sierra Nevadas,
in the long azure of your wife's glance,
in the roads and the standing water,
in the trembling of a spider web gone suddenly still,
it never happened.

12.

This is a good page.
It is blank,
and getting blanker.
My mother and father
are falling asleep over it.
My brother is finishing a cigarette;
he looks at the blank moon.
My sisters walk gravely in circles.
My wife sees through it, through blankness.
My friends stop laughing, they listen
to the wind in a room in Fresno, to the wind
of this page, which is theirs,
which is blank.

They are all tired of reading,
they want to go home,
they won't be waving goodbye.

When they are gone,
the page will be crumpled,
thrown into the street.
Around it, sparrows will be feeding
on bits of garbage.
The linnet will be singing.
A man will awaken on his deathbed,
not yet cured.

I will not have written these words,
I will be that silence slipping around the bend
in the river, where it curves out of sight among weeds,
the silence in which a car backfires and drives away,
and the father of that silence.

The Dollmaker's Ghost

Picking grapes alone in the late autumn sun—
A short, curved knife in my hand,
Its blade silver from so many sharpenings,
Its handle black.
I still have a scar where a friend
Sliced open my right index finger, once,
In a cutting shed—
The same kind of knife.
The grapes drop into the pan,
And the gnats swarm over them, as always.
Fifteen years ago,
I worked this row of vines beside a dozen
Families up from Mexico.
No one spoke English, or wanted to.
One woman, who made an omelet with a sheet of tin
And five, light blue quail eggs,
Had a voice full of dusk, and jail cells,
And bird calls.   She spoke,
In Spanish, to no one, as they all did.
Their swearing was specific,
And polite.
I remember two of them clearly:
A man named Tea, six feet, nine inches tall
At the age of sixty-two,
Who wore white spats into downtown Fresno
Each Saturday night,
An alcoholic giant whom the women loved—
One chilled morning, they found him dead outside
The Rose Café . . .
And Angel Domínguez,
Who came to work for my grandfather in 1910,
And who saved for years to buy
Twenty acres of rotting, Thompson Seedless vines.
While the sun flared all one August,

He decided he was dying of a rare disease,
And spent his money and his last years
On specialists,
Who found nothing wrong.
Tea laughed, and, tipping back
A bottle of Muscatel, said: "Nothing's wrong.
You're just dying."
At seventeen, I discovered
Parlier, California, with its sad, topless bar,
And its one main street, and its opium.
I would stand still, and chalk my cue stick
In Johnny Palores' East Front Pool Hall, and watch
The room filling with tobacco smoke, as the sun set
Through one window.
Now all I hear are the vines rustling as I go
From one to the next,
The long canes holding up dry leaves, reddening,
So late in the year.
What the vines want must be this silence spreading
Over each town, over the dance halls and the dying parks,
And the police drowsing in their cruisers
Under the stars.
What the men who worked here wanted was
A drink strong enough
To let out what laughter they had.
I can still see the two of them:
Tea smiles and lets his yellow teeth shine—
While Angel, the serious one, for whom
Death was a rare disease,
Purses his lips, and looks down, as if
He is already mourning himself—
A soft, gray hat between his hands.
Today, in honor of them,
I press my thumb against the flat part of this blade,
And steady a bunch of red, Málaga grapes
With one hand,

The way they showed me, and cut—
And close my eyes to hear them laugh at me again,
And then, hearing nothing, no one,
Carry the grapes up to the solemn house,
Where I was born.

1.

After five years,
I'm in the kitchen of my parents' house
Again, hearing the aging refrigerator
Go on with its music,
And watching an insect die on the table
By turning in circles.
My face reflected in the window at night
Is paler, duller, even in summer.
And each year
I dislike sleeping a little more,
And all the hours spent
Inside something as black
As my own skull . . .
I watch
This fruit moth flutter.
Now it's stopped.

2.

Once,
Celebrating a good year for Muscatel,
My parents got away to Pismo Beach,
Shuttered and cold in the off season.
When I stare out at its surf at night,
It could be a girl in a black and white slip,
It could be nothing.
But I no longer believe this is where
America ends.   I know
It continues as oil, or sorrow, or a tiny
Island with palm trees lining
The sun baked, crumbling
Asphalt of its airstrip.
A large snake sleeps in the middle of it,
And it is not necessary to think of war,

Or the isolation of any father
Alone on a raft in the Pacific
At night, or how deep the water can get
Beneath him . . .
Not when I can think of the look of distance
That must have spread
Over my parents' faces as they
Conceived me here,
And each fell back, alone,
As the waves glinted, and fell back.

3.
This evening my thoughts
Build one white bridge after another
Into the twilight, and now the tiny couple
In the distance,
In the picture I have of them there,
This woman pregnant after a war,
And this man who whistles with a dog at his heels,
And who thinks all this is his country,
Cross over them without
Looking back, without waving.
Already, in the orchards behind them,
The solitary hives are things;
They have the dignity of things,
A gray, precise look,
While the new wasps swarm sullenly out of them,
And the trees hold up cold blossoms,
And, in the distance, the sky
Does not mind the one bird in it,
Which by now is only a frail brush stroke
On a canvas in which everything is muted and
Real.   The way laughter is real
When it ends, suddenly, between two strangers,
And you step quickly past them, into the night.

**To a Wall of Flame in a Steel Mill,
Syracuse, New York, 1969**

Except under the cool shadows of pines,
The snow is already thawing
Along this road . . .
Such sun, and wind.
I think my father longed to disappear
While driving through this place once,
In 1957.
Beside him, my mother slept in a gray dress
While his thoughts moved like the shadow
Of a cloud over houses,
And he was seized, suddenly, by his own shyness,
By his desire to be grass,
And simplified.
Was it brought on
By the road, or the snow, or the sky
With nothing in it?
He kept sweating and wiping his face
Until it passed,
And I never knew.
But in the long journey away from my father,
I took only his silences, his indifference
To misfortune, rain, stones, music, and grief.
Now, I can sleep beside this road
If I have to,
Even while the stars pale and go out,
And it is day.
And if I can keep secrets for years,
The way a stone retains a warmth from the sun,
It is because men like us
Own nothing, really.
I remember, once,
In the steel mill where I worked,
Someone opened the door of the furnace

And I glanced in at the simple,
Quick and blank erasures the flames made of iron,
Of everything on earth.
It was reverence I felt then, and did not know why.
I do not know even now why my father
Lived out his one life
Farming two hundred acres of gray Málaga vines
And peach trees twisted
By winter.   They lived, I think,
Because his hatred of them was entire,
And wordless.
I still think of him staring into this road
Twenty years ago,
While his hands gripped the wheel harder,
And his wish to be no one made his body tremble,
Like the touch
Of a woman he could not see,
Her fingers drifting up his spine in silence
Until his loneliness was perfect,
And she let him go—
Her laughter turning into these sheets of black
And glassy ice that dislodge themselves,
And ride slowly out,
Onto the thawing river.

Truman, Da Vinci, Nebraska

In Kansas City, Truman is dead who ruled
In green Missouris of decisive, late
Spring nights and wet roads somebody had
To die on: between Rolla and Joplin for

A wisecrack, or a girl who stole convertibles
For thrills.   At the end I thought he'd
Plant tiny, American flags in no wind, in his
Coma, his Asia.   But no.   At the end his face

In the newspapers smeared with rain still
Looked delicately cross with something, almost
Childish, tired. The waitress in this truck stop
Believes, with Da Vinci, that the world would end

In fires, storms, and silence.   This is Nebraska,
Where the cattle across from us look up quietly,
Chewing sideways with abrupt motions.   I watch
A whole weed, roots and all, disappear.   It was

Da Vinci who knew all the muscles in the human face.

The young woman is just sitting on the bed,
Looking down.   The room is so narrow she keeps
Her elbows tucked in, resting, on her bare thighs,
As if that could help.

She is wearing, now, only an orange half-slip
That comes down as far as her waist, but does not
Console her body, which fails.
Which must sleep, by now, apart from everyone.
And her face, in shadow,
Is more silent than this painting, or any
Painting: it feels like the sad, blank hull
Of a ship is passing, slowly, the stones of a wharf,
Though there is no ocean for a thousand miles,
And outside this room I can imagine only Kansas:
Its wheat, and blackening silos, and, beyond that,
The plains that will stare back at you until
The day your mother, kneeling in fumes
On a hardwood floor, begins to laugh out loud.
When you visit her, you see the same, faint grass
Around the edge of the asylum, and a few moths,
White and flagrant, against the wet brick there,
Where she has gone to live.   She never
Recognizes you again.

You sell the house, and auction off each thing
Inside the house, until
You have a satchel, a pair of black, acceptable
Shoes, and one good flowered dress.   There is a check
Between your hands and your bare knees for all of it—
The land and the wheat that never cared who
Touched it, or why.

You think of curves, of the slow, mild arcs
Of harbors in California: Half Moon Bay,

Malibu, names that seem to undress
When you say them, beaches that stay white
Until you get there.   Still, you're only thirty-five,
And that is not too old to be a single woman,
Traveling west with a purse in her gray lap
Until all of Kansas dies inside her stare . . .

But you never moved, never roused yourself
To go down Grain Street to the sobering station,
Never gazed out at the raw tracks, and waited
For the train that pushed its black smoke up
Into the sky like something important . . .

And now it is too late for you.   Now no one,
Turning his collar up against the cold
To walk past the first, full sunlight flooding
The white sides of houses, knows why
You've kept on sitting here for forty years—alone,
Almost left out of the picture, half undressed.

for D. J.

10 p.m., the river thinking
Of its last effects,
The bridges empty.   I think
You would have left the party late,

Declining a ride home.
And no one notices, now,
The moist hat brims
Between the thumbs of farmers

In Beatrice, Nebraska.
The men in their suits,
Ill fitting, bought on sale . . .
The orange moon of foreclosures.

And abandoning the car!
How you soloed, finally,
Lending it the fabulous touch
Of your absence.

You'd call that style—
To stand with an unlit cigarette
In one corner of your mouth,
Admiring the sun on Alcatraz.

For Miguel Hernández in His Sleep and in His Sickness: Spring, 1942, Madrid

You have slept for two days now,
And still you do not want
To die in here.
If you had a choice,
You would lie without thoughts in the long grass,
Where the grass is whitest—
Each blade of it a flame that says nothing,
That loves nothing . . .
If you had a choice,
You would be done with loving forever.
You would walk toward a loud square in Madrid,
And lie down, unnoticed, in the twisting shade
Of a black tree, and sleep.
Or maybe you would only pretend to sleep—
Maybe you would close your eyes in the sun,
And let the flies settle on your lips,
And listen to the threadbare blood rushing
Inside your veins;
Maybe you would let the stray goats nuzzle your hands,
Since there is nothing shameful
Under the sky.
But on the third day
Without food, or prayers, or water,
You would see your first and last words grow still
As a glass of wine in a woman's hand:
She would be sitting in a café, alone,
Not noticing you, not
Hearing your breath become quick and shallow—
Until finally you would let it all out in one hard laugh
That withers quickly
Into the noise of the street.
And without breath,
You would become the street:

You would become these goats braying,
The scrape of soldiers,
A girl's laugh inside a bar . . .
I could visit you years from now
In these bricks and these black shops and even
In this shattered glass that no one cleans up,
That shines in the sun—
That remains
When everyone goes home to curse, or sleep,
Or lie awake between his own two hands.
And who knows how this night will end?
The grass stirs once and stills
Outside the prison.
You think no one is worth his life, and the stars,
Even the rare, white ones that are so useless
To men and women,
Show up again above you.

No matter how hard I listen, the wind speaks
One syllable, which has no comfort in it—
Only a rasping of air through the dead elm.

Once a poet told me of his friend who was torn apart
By two pigs in a field in Poland. The man
Was a prisoner of the Nazis, and they watched,
He said, with interest and a drunken approval . . .
If terror is a state of complete understanding,

Then there was probably a point at which the man
Went mad, and felt nothing, though certainly
He understood everything that was there: after all,
He could see blood splash beneath him on the stubble,
He could hear singing float toward him from the barracks.

And though I don't know much about madness,
I know it lives in the thin body like a harp
Behind the rib cage.   It makes it painful to move.
And when you kneel in madness your knees are glass,
And so you must stand up again with great care.

Maybe this wind was what he heard in 1941.
Maybe I have raised a dead man into this air,
And now I will have to bury him inside my body,
And breathe him in, and do nothing but listen—
Until I hear the black blood rushing over
The stone of my skull, and believe it is music.

But some things are not possible on the earth.
And that is why people make poems about the dead.
And the dead watch over them, until they are finished:
Until their hands feel like glass on the page,
And snow collects in the blind eyes of statues.

García Lorca: A Photograph of the Granada Cemetery, 1966

The men who killed poetry
Hated silence . . . Now they have plenty.
In the ossuary at Granada
There are over four thousand calm skulls
Whitening; the shrubs are in leaf
Behind the bones.
And if anyone tries to count spines
He can feel his own scalp start to crawl
Back to its birthplace.

Once, I gave you a small stone I respected.
When I turned it over in the dawn,
After staying up all night,
Its pale depths
Resembled the tense face of Lorca
Spitting into an empty skull.
Why did he do that?
Someone should know.
Someone should know by now that the stone
Was only an amulet to keep the dead away.

And though your long bones
Have nothing to do with Lorca, or those deaths
Forty years ago, in Spain,
The trees fill with questions, and summer.
He would not want, tonight, another elegy.
He would want me to examine the marriage of wings
Beneath your delicate collar bones:
They breathe,
The ribs of your own poems breathe.

And here is our dark house at the end of the lane.
And here is the one light we have kept on all year
For no one, or Lorca,
And now he comes toward it—
With the six bulletholes in his chest,
Walking lightly
So he will not disturb the sleeping neighbors,
Or the almonds withering in their frail arks
Above us.
He does not want to come in.
He stands embarrassed under the street lamp
In his rumpled suit . . .

Snow, lullabye, anvil of bone
That terrifies the blacksmith in his sleep,

Your house is breath.

In Fresno it is 1923, and your shy father
Has picked up a Chinese fan abandoned
Among the corsages crushed into the dance floor.
On it, a man with scrolls is crossing a rope bridge
Over gradually whitening water.
If you look closely you can see brush strokes intended
To be trout.
You can see that the whole scene
Is centuries older
Than the hotel, or Fresno in the hard glare of morning.
And the girl
Who used this fan to cover her mouth
Or breasts under the cool brilliance
Of chandeliers
Is gone on a train sliding along tracks that are
Pitted with rust.
All this is taking her south,
And as your father opens the fan now you can see
The rope bridge tremble and the lines of concentration
Come over the face of this thin scholar
Who makes the same journey alone each year
Into the high passes,
Who sleeps on the frozen ground, hearing the snow
Melt around him as he tries hard
Not to be involved with it, not to be
Awakened by a spring that was never meant
To include him—
And though he hears the geese racket above him
As if a stick were held flat against
A slat fence by a child running past a house for sale;
And though he has seen his sons' kites climb the air
With clumsy animals, dragons and oxen,
Painted over them in great detail,
He does not care if kites continue to stiffen

Each year against the sky, the sun.
When he lays
His one good ear to the ground he thinks
He is the conclusion of something argued over all night,
He thinks of his skull as a drum with a split skin
Left out in the rain,
Washed continually but not about to be picked up
As someone picks up a fan even, out of curiosity,
Revolves it slowly,
And now, gently closes it.
And though flies cover the chandeliers this morning,
The new seeds steam underground,
The snow melts,
The mist rises off the thawing river,
And the girl wakens in her berth—
Her face cradling a slight frown,
As if she had just outgrown all dancing,
And turned serious, like the sky.

There is still one field I can love;
There is still a little darkness in each furrow
And each stump.
Behind it
You can sit down and begin to doubt
Even the hair on the backs of your hands—
And what you see now is nothing:
It is only
The scrubbed, wooden sink inside this shack
Abandoned by farm workers,
Or, above a kitchen window, only a strip of curtain
Which is the color of no flag
And no country, though once it meant *night*—
And so the occupant stared out at the sky whitening
Into each dawn—
At all the withheld information
Which is sky,
And thought if he worked all day to shovel
Thirty acres of vines
Without once looking up into those torn clouds,
If he could sweat past such insolence into nightfall,
And ignore that, too, until he saw her
Turning from a bath,
Her skin suddenly
There, and darker than he could have believed—
As if night had entered the dusk
Of her body . . .
So their eyes and mouths opened, then.

And now,
If we listen for their laughter,
Which vanished fifteen years ago
Into the cleft wood of these boards,
Into the night and the rain,

It will sound like cold jewels spilling together,
It will sound like snow . . .
We will never have any money, either,
And we will go on staring past the sink,
Past the curtain,
And into a field which is not even white anymore,
Not even an orchard,
But simply this mud,
And always,
Over that, a hard sky.
And what I have to tell you now is only
The salt that ripens in our passing, and
Overwhelms us:
How I heard, once,
Of two lovers, who
Naked, and for a joke,
Tied themselves together with cast off clothes
And leaped into a canal—
Where the current held them under a whole hour.
I thought, then,
How each of them must have said all that can
Be said
Between a man and a woman—
As they fought each other to breathe,
Or, which is the same thing,
To be whole, and lonely again.
But I was wrong:
They only stiffened, and there were no words left
Inside them—
The man lay face down in the stillness;
The woman faced the sky.
Bobbing in the thick grass beside the banks,
Their arms whitened around each other for three days
In the stale water . . .
Now they are these words.
And now, if I strike a match
To offer you
This page burned all the way

Into their silences,
Take it—
While your hair dies a little more
Into the day,
While the sun rises,
These two will be ashes in the palm of my hand,
Stirring a little and about to drift
Easily away, without comment,
On the wind.

To become as pure as I am,
You will have to sit all day in a small park
Blackening one end of Fowler, California.
You will have to stare steadily past the still swings
Ignored by children,
And listen to the perfect Spanish of a car thief
Who knows he will never be caught,
Who drinks wine alone as he mumbles his innocence
To a dead sister.
You will have to study the muscles in the face of a woman
Sickened by no one, or summer, who pulls a shopping cart
Behind her with a black, gloved hand.
Each day she pauses before going up
The slope of the hill.
She complains to her three distinct, personal gods,
She wets her lips,
She almost dozes on her feet.
The car thief takes a long sip of wine and watches her,
And watches the shadows falling over the swings,
And the shrubs, and the sparrows.
Again today I bet against the shadows and lost:
They lengthened
For hours until their immaculate shade
Contradicted the sky.
And though it is the same sky the two lovers sat under,
They were so undone by their own glances,
By the white silks of their flesh,
I almost believed I was wrong about this place.
In my silence, of course, I bet against them,
And bet too hard.
As summer worried the lace from ferns,
And as summer nights rotted the eyes out of moths,
In August,
I watched the boy stifle a yawn,

I watched them quarrel.
Soon the girl was just something thin in a blue dress,
Sitting alone in shade.
The woman in black gloves is too old to care
About shade now.
She stands out on the sidewalk and lets the heat
Pour through her, and lets the muscles of her heart
Learn what the sun can do.
And if she laughs,
It is because the humiliation of sunlight
Has cured her body of every dignity,
And made it useless again.
To become this pure, this empty,
You will have to sit beside me for hours,
And hear the car thief explain his crime over and over,
Or watch this woman pray against the muscles
Inside her own mind,
And then follow her up the hill
Until she disappears,
And you find only yourself staring back
At the green shadows spreading through the park, and the shrubs
Refusing to die, and the three motionless swings.

The Missouri is only a mile from this place,
But I haven't seen it glint through the bridge railings
For two months, its back careless, flat,
And unaging.
Seen for the first time it moves faster
Than you expected, like the back
Of an animal you glimpse from the highway
But can't identify.
And once, on its banks near Canada,
I saw a bear
Moving quickly through goldenrod glance up once
And judge me.   Then it
Walked off with a sort of arrogant peacefulness
In each stride.
And held for a moment in the contempt
Of its stare, hearing
The wind over the blind stones,
I learned only what I knew:
That the sun would go down,
The bread I was eating would be water,
And the river would flow under the creaking pilings
Until another shack came riding high
In the spring floods.
And trapped twice by rising water,
I was lucky enough to crawl into a cave and share it
With scorpions, and admire their selfishness,
And bless power.

But nothing could laugh fear out of my house—
It lived in the brown shoes I had to put on
Each morning, and in the cancer blooming under
My father's lapel, and in my mother taking in laundry
All through World War I.

Fear was curious: it asked me
My name, asked me to sit down and showed me all the tools
In the shed, and asked me if I knew their uses.
And I lied because I needed the money;
And because they said someone had to place buttons
Carefully in the skulls of dolls,
And do this over and over,
I was a dollmaker.
Until each doll grew luminous, and each inhaled
My gaze. And then I gave those eyes
Everything they asked,
Which was nothing.
Which was thirty years.

And once, driving home, I saw a torn mattress
High on a riverbank, and wondered
Who had slept there, what love stains
Might be drying on it in the late afternoon sun,
And what lice might be sleeping inside it,
Unaware that their hosts had moved elsewhere.
And so strapped it over the roof of my car,
And got it home,
And sat there on it, drinking wine and grinning.
And it was my wide grin and all 29 teeth
That remembered who I had slept with
In 1947, and who was
Blinded at random on the street by acid thrown
Into her eyes,
And why the sky is for sale.
Because in the end it wasn't a bear
Or a mattress on a raft that saved me.
It wasn't my body
Like a graveyard glimpsed inside a sunset
While someone is writing a letter;
It wasn't even my disappearance,
Or my cousins dredging the water.

It was the river moving all night under me,
It was the fast, black river
That didn't care what I did,
That slowed when I looked at it closely
And carried twigs and shoes
And a rank stench like unwashed human hair and flesh
Past the abandoned freight yards of the Missouri,
And past the white hair of women who go mad on its banks,
Watching for my body to surface in the warming water.

And now I will sit here all night carving
At a dry stick of wood,
Ignoring whoever it is
That gets up slowly and walks back
To his car, and rolls up the windows—
So he won't hear the grass dying around me
In late August—
And drives away.

Blue Stones

for my son, Nicholas

I suspect
They will slide me onto a cold bed,
A bed that has been brought in,
Out of the night
And past the fraying brick of the warehouse,
Where maybe a workman took an afternoon nap,
And woke staring up
At what sky he could see through one window.
But if he kept staring,
And thought that the bed took its gray color
From the sky, and kept watching that sky
Even after he had finished his cigarette,
He might learn
How things outlive us.
And maybe he would be reminded that the body, too
Is only a thing, a joke it kept trying to tell us,
And now the moment for hearing it
Is past.
All I will have to decide, then,
Is how to behave during
Those last weeks, when the drawers
Of the dresser remain closed,
And the mirror is calm, and reflects nothing,
And outside, tangled
In the hard branches,
The moon appears.
I see how poor it is,
How it owns nothing.
I look at it a long time, until
I feel empty, as if I had travelled on foot
For three days, and become simple,
The way light was simple on the backs
Of horses as my father approached them,

Quietly, with a bridle.
My father thought dying
Was like standing trial for crimes
You could not remember.
Then someone really does throw
The first stone.
It is blue,
And seems to be made of the sky itself.
The breath goes out of you.
Tonight, the smoke holds still
Against the hills and trees outside this town,
And there is no hope
Of acquittal.

But *you?* Little believer, little
Straight, unbroken, and tireless thing,
Someday, when you are twenty-four and walking through
The streets of a foreign city, Stockholm,
Or Trieste,
Let me go with you a little way,
Let me be that stranger you won't notice,
And when you turn and enter a bar full of young men
And women, and your laughter rises,
Like the stones of a path up a mountain,
To say that no one has died,
I promise I will not follow.
I will cross at the corner in my gray sweater.
I will not have touched you,
As I did, for so many years,
On the hair and the left shoulder.
I will silence my hand that wanted to.
I will put it in my pocket, and let it clutch
The cold, blue stones they give you,
As a punishment,
After you have lived.

Because you haven't praised anything in months,
You walk down to the river and study one ripple
Above a dead tree
Until it is almost dark enough
For the moon to whiten it,
But it does not,
And so you put your hand out,
Palm open,
And then you feel, or you begin to feel,
A thin line of ants hesitate
Before running over it,
And you think how
The thread of worry running through a human voice
Halts when a syllable freezes, then goes on,
Alone.   You remember
Overhearing two voices speak softly
In a motel room.
Outside, it was 1975,
And cars sighed past weeds, and fields.
You think now they were only
A man and a woman consoling each other
Because they had both
Lived out their lives, and there was no point
Anymore worth arguing, even if once
There was something, no money, or a daughter
Staying out all night even on the blackest night
Of summer, and coming home
Whitened and final as snow in the back seat
Of a convertible—
The car abandoned, by now, to the sky and the sun—
But no, they
Were just consoling each other
For being who they were,
And because they could not change,

Not now, into
Anything else.
And because one day one of them will simply look over
To see if the water on the stove
Is boiling, and if it is clear, finally,
Of the gray, shifting sky it had reflected
A moment ago,
And then he, or she, will be alone—
Though the sun might move to illuminate
A spiked clematis on the windowsill,
Which will be too revealing.
And whoever is left
Will begin to know what it is like
To take one step slowly backward;
To be without a voice to sort the mind
As it begins, now, to flare like the horns
Of a marching band coming up the street under
The elms;

To feel a slight wind stirring the hair at the back
Of the neck . . .

To stand there.

By now you are lying so still
You think you can rise up, as I can,
Without a body,
And go unseen over the still heads of grasses,
And enter the house
Where your wife will not look up from the letter
She is writing,
And your son goes on sleeping—
A thimble of light spilling into the darkness.
But you do not move.   And this
Is about stillness, now:
How you remember strolling alone, at seventeen,

Through the dusk of each street,
How you liked the wind reddening the face
Of a drunk, who,
In the last days of his alcohol, reeled
And stared back at you,
And held your gaze.
How all you remember of New York is
That man,
Who would not have read this poem,
Or any poem,
And who once dreamed
That a speck of white paint on a subway platform
Would outlast
Everyone he knew.

But you were young, and you had
Plenty of time:
Going west,

You slept on the train and did not smile.
Under you the plains widened, and turned silver.

You slept with your mouth open.

You were nothing,
You were snow falling through the ribs
Of the dead.

You were all I had.

Winter Stars

The Poet at Seventeen

My youth? I hear it mostly in the long, volleying
Echoes of billiards in the pool halls where
I spent it all, extravagantly, believing
My delicate touch on a cue would last for years.

Outside the vineyards vanished under rain,
And the trees held still or seemed to hold their breath
When the men I worked with, pruning orchards, sang
Their lost songs: *Amapola; La Paloma;*

Jalisco, No Te Rajes—the corny tunes
Their sons would just as soon forget, at recess,
Where they lounged apart in small groups of their own.
Still, even when they laughed, they laughed in Spanish.

I hated high school then, & on weekends drove
A tractor through the widowed fields. It was so boring
I memorized poems above the engine's monotone.
Sometimes whole days slipped past without my noticing,

And birds of all kinds flew in front of me then.
I learned to tell them apart by their empty squabblings,
The slightest change in plumage, or the inflection
Of a call. And why not admit it? I was happy

Then. I believed in no one. I had the kind
Of solitude the world usually allows
Only to kings & criminals who are extinct,
Who disdain this world, & who rot, corrupt & shallow

As fields I disced: I turned up the same gray
Earth for years. Still, the land made a glum raisin
Each autumn, & made that little hell of days—
The vines must have seemed like cages to the Mexicans

Who were paid seven cents a tray for the grapes
They picked. Inside the vines it was hot, & spiders
Strummed their emptiness. Black Widow, Daddy Longlegs.
The vine canes whipped our faces. None of us cared.

And the girls I tried to talk to after class
Sailed by, then each night lay enthroned in my bed,
With nothing on but the jewels of their embarrassment.
Eyes, lips, dreams. No one. The sky & the road.

A life like that? It seemed to go on forever—
Reading poems in school, then driving a stuttering tractor
Warm afternoons, then billiards on blue October
Nights. The thick stars. But mostly now I remember

The trees, wearing their mysterious yellow sullenness
Like party dresses. And parties I didn't attend.
And then the first ice hung like spider lattices
Or the embroideries of Great Aunt No One,

And then the first dark entering the trees—
And inside, the adults with their cocktails before dinner,
The way they always seemed afraid of something,
And sat so rigidly, although the land was theirs.

Adolescence

for Sharon and Earl

Our babysitter lives across from the Dodge Street cemetery,
And behind her broad, untroubled face.
Her sons play touch football all afternoon
Among the graves of clerks & Norwegian settlers.
At night, these huge trees, rooted in such quiet,
Arch over the tombstones as if in exultation,
As if they inhaled starlight.
Their limbs reach
Toward each other & their roots must touch the dead.

When I was fifteen,
There was a girl who loved me; whom I did not love, & she
Died, that year, of spinal meningitis. By then she
Had already left home, & was working in a carnival—
One of those booths where you are supposed
To toss a dime onto a small dish. Finally,
In Laredo, Texas, someone anonymous, & too late, bought her
A bus ticket back. . . .
Her father, a gambler & horse dealer, wept
Openly the day she was buried. I remember looking off
In embarrassment at the woods behind his house.
The woods were gray, vagrant, the color of smoke
Or sky. I remember thinking then that
If I had loved her, or even slept with her once,
She might still be alive.
And if, instead, we had gone away together
On two bay horses that farted when they began to gallop,
And if, later, we had let them
Graze at their leisure on the small tufts of spring grass
In those woods, & if the disintegrating print of the ferns
Had been a lullaby there against the dry stones & the trunks
Of fallen trees, then maybe nothing would have happened. . . .
There are times, hiking with my wife past

Abandoned orchards of freckled apples & patches of sunlight
In New Hampshire, or holding her closely against me at night
Until she sleeps, when nothing else matters, when
The trees shine without meaning more than they are, in moonlight,
And when it seems possible to disappear wholly into someone
Else, as into a wish on a birthday, the candles trembling . . .

Maybe nothing would have happened, but I heard that
Her father died, a year later, in a Sierra lumber camp.
He had been drinking steadily all week,
And was dealing cards
When the muscle of his own heart
Kicked him back into his chair so hard its wood snapped.
He must have thought there was something
Suddenly very young inside his body,
If he had time to think. . . .
And if death is an adolescent, closing his eyes to the music
On the radio of that passing car,
I think he does not know his own strength.
If I stand here long enough in this stillness I can feel
His silence involve, somehow, the silence of these trees,
The sky, the little squawking toy my son lost
When it slipped into the river today. . . .
Today, I am thirty-four years old. I know
That horse dealer with a limp loved his plain, & crazy daughter.
I know, also, that it did no good.
Soon, the snows will come again & cover that place
Where he sat at a wobbling card table underneath
A Ponderosa pine, & cover
Even the three cards he dropped there, three silent diamonds,
And cover everything in the Sierras, & make my meaning plain.

Then, everything slept.
The sky & the fields slept all the way to the Pacific,
And the houses slept.
The orchards blackened in their sleep,
And, outside my window, the aging Palomino slept
Standing up in the moonlight, with one rear hoof slightly cocked,
And the moonlight slept.
The white dust slept between the rows of vines,
And the quail slept perfectly, like untouched triangles.
The hawk slept alone, apart from this world.
In the distance I could see the faint glow
Of Parlier—even its name a lullaby,
Where the little bars slept with only one light on,
And the prostitutes slept, as always,
With the small-time businessmen, their hair smelling of pomade,
Who did not dream.
Dice slept in the hands of the town's one gambler, & outside
His window, the brown grass slept,
And beyond that, in a low stand of trees, ashes slept
Where men with no money had built a fire, and lain down,
Beside the river,
And saw in their sleep how the cold shape of fire
Made, from each crystal of ash, the gray morning,
Which consoled no one.
Beside me, my brother slept
With a small frown knitted into his face, as if
He listened for something, his mouth open.
But there was nothing.
On my last night as a child, that sleep was final.
Above me, the shingles slept on the roof,
And the brick chimney, with smoke rising through it, slept,
And the notes on sheet music slept.
I went downstairs, then, to the room
Where my mother & father slept with nothing on, & the pale light

Shone through the window on the candor
Of their bodies strewn over the sheets, & those bodies
Were not beautiful, like distant cities.
They were real bodies
With bruises & lattices of fatigue over their white stomachs,
And over their faces.
His hair was black, & thinning. Hers was the color of ashes.
I could see every detail that disappointment had sketched,
Idly, into them: her breasts & the widening thigh
That mocked my mother with the intricate,
Sorrowing spasm of birth;
I could see
The stooped shoulders & sunken chest of my father,
Sullen as the shape of a hawk in wet weather,
The same shape it takes in its death,
When you hold it in your outstretched hand,
And wonder how it can shrink to so small a thing,
And then you are almost afraid, judging by the truculence
Of its beak & the vast, intricate plan
Of its color & delicate shading, black & red & white,
That it is only sleeping,
Only pretending a death.
But both of them really unlike anything else
Unless you thought, as I did,
Of the shape of beaten snow, & absence, & a sleep
Without laughter.
They lay there on their bed.
I saw every detail, & as I turned away
Those bodies moved slightly in the languor of sleep,
And my mother cried out once, but did not awaken,
And that cry stayed on in the air—
And even as I turned away, their frail bodies,
Seen as if for a last time,
Reminded me of ravines on either side of the road,
When I ran,
And did not know why.

My father once broke a man's hand
Over the exhaust pipe of a John Deere tractor. The man,
Rubén Vásquez, wanted to kill his own father
With a sharpened fruit knife, & he held
The curved tip of it, lightly, between his first
Two fingers, so it could slash
Horizontally, & with surprising grace,
Across a throat. It was like a glinting beak in a hand,
And, for a moment, the light held still
On those vines. When it was over,
My father simply went in & ate lunch, & then, as always,
Lay alone in the dark, listening to music.
He never mentioned it.

I never understood how anyone could risk his life,
Then listen to Vivaldi.

Sometimes, I go out into this yard at night,
And stare through the wet branches of an oak
In winter, & realize I am looking at the stars
Again. A thin haze of them, shining
And persisting.

It used to make me feel lighter, looking up at them.
In California, that light was closer.
In a California no one will ever see again,
My father is beginning to die. Something
Inside him is slowly taking back
Every word it ever gave him.
Now, if we try to talk, I watch my father
Search for a lost syllable as if it might
Solve everything, & though he can't remember, now,
The word for it, he is ashamed. . . .
If you can think of the mind as a place continually

Visited, a whole city placed behind
The eyes, & shining, I can imagine, now, its end—
As when the lights go off, one by one,
In a hotel at night, until at last
All of the travelers will be asleep, or until
Even the thin glow from the lobby is a kind
Of sleep; & while the woman behind the desk
Is applying more lacquer to her nails,
You can almost believe that the elevator,
As it ascends, must open upon starlight.

I stand out on the street, & do not go in.
That was our agreement, at my birth.

And for years I believed
That what went unsaid between us became empty,
And pure, like starlight, & that it persisted.

I got it all wrong.
I wound up believing in words the way a scientist
Believes in carbon, after death.

Tonight, I'm talking to you, father, although
It is quiet here in the Midwest, where a small wind,
The size of a wrist, wakes the cold again—
Which may be all that's left of you & me.

When I left home at seventeen, I left for good.

The pale haze of stars goes on & on,
Like laughter that has found a final, silent shape
On a black sky. It means everything
It cannot say. Look, it's empty out there, & cold.
Cold enough to reconcile
Even a father, even a son.

Now in middle age, my blood like a thief who
Got away, unslain, & the trees hung again in the grim,
Cheap embroidery of leaves, I come back to the white roads,
The intersections in their sleeves of dust,
And vines like woodwinds twisted into shapes
For playing different kinds of silence.
Just when my hearing was getting perfect, singular
As an orphan's shard of mirror, they
Change the music into something I
No longer follow.
But how like them to welcome me home this way:
The house with its doorstep finally rotted away,
And carted off for a stranger's firewood,
And yet, behind the window there,
A woman bent over a map of her childhood, but still
A real map, that shows her people's
Ireland like a bonnet for the mad on top of
Plenty of ocean.
Hunger kept those poor relations traveling until
They almost touched the sea again,
And settled.
And there have been changes, even here.
In Parlier, California,
The band in the park still plays the same song,
But with a fresher strain of hopelessness.
This, too, will pass.
That is the message, always, of its threadbare refrain,
The message, too, of what one chooses to forget
About this place: the Swedish tailgunner who,
After twenty missions in the Pacific, chopped off
His own left hand
To get back home. No one thinks of him;

Not even I believe he found another reason, maybe,
For all left hands. So memory sires
Oblivion—this settlement of sheds, & weeds,
Where the last exile which the bloodstream always sang
Comes down to a matter of a few sparrows hopping
On & off a broken rain gutter, or downspout, & behind them,
A barn set up on a hill & meant to stay there,
Ignoring the sky
With the certainty they bolted into the crossbeams—
The whole thing
Towering over the long silent
Farmer & his wife; & that still house
Where their fingers have remembered, for fifty years,
Just where to touch the bannister; & then the steps,
That, one day, led up to me. Come home,
Say the blackened, still standing chimneys, & the missing bell
Above the three-room schoolhouse—
You've inherited all there is: the ironic,
Rueful smile of a peasant who's extinct,
Who nods, understanding, too well, the traveler,
And who orders another shot of schnapps
While his wife, pregnant, angry, puts both hands
Under her chin, & waits up.

And always, I pack the car, I answer no. . . .
When my own son was next to nothing,
He, too, would wait up with us,
Awake with hands already wholly formed,
And no larger than twin question marks in the book I closed,
One day, in a meadow,
When I reached for her—above the silent town,
Above the gray, decaying smoke of the vineyards.

A stranger who saw us there might have said:
I saw two people naked on your land.
But afterward, our pulses
Already lulling & growing singular, my eyes
Closed on that hill, I saw
A playground, mothers chatting; water falling because
It was right to *be* falling, over a cliff; & the way
Time & the lights of all home towns grew still
In that tense shape of water just before it fell . . .
I watched it a long time,
And, for no reason I could name, turned away from it,
To take that frail path along a mountainside—
Then passed through alder, spruce, & stunted pine,
Stone & a cold wind,
Up to the empty summit.

Dressed to die...

—Dylan Thomas

Sister once of weeds & a dark water that held still
In ditches reflecting the odd,
Abstaining clouds that passed, & kept
Their own counsel, we
Were different, we kept our own counsel.
Outside the tool shed in the noon heat, while our father
Ground some piece of metal
That would finally fit, with grease & an hour of pushing,
The needs of the mysterious Ford tractor,
We argued out, in adolescence,
Whole systems of mathematics, ethics,
And finally agreed that *altruism,*
Whose long vowel sounded like pigeons,
Roosting stupidly & about to be shot
In the barn, was impossible
If one was born a Catholic. The Swedish
Lutherans, whom the nuns called
"Statue smashers," the Japanese on
Neighboring farms, were, we guessed,
A little better off. . . .
When I was twelve, I used to stare at weeds
Along the road, at the way they kept trembling
Long after a car had passed;
Or at gnats in families hovering over
Some rotting peaches, & wonder why it was
I had been born a human.
Why not a weed, or a gnat?
Why not a horse, or a spider? And why an American?
I did not think that anything could choose me
To be a Larry Levis before there even *was*

A Larry Levis. It was strange, but not strange enough
To warrant some design.
                              On the outside,
The barn, with flaking paint, was still off-white.
Inside, it was always dark, all the way up
To the rafters where the pigeons moaned,
I later thought, as if in sexual complaint,
Or sexual abandon; I never found out which.
When I walked in with a 12-gauge & started shooting,
They fell, like gray fruit, at my feet—
Fat, thumping things that grew quieter
When their eyelids, a softer gray, closed,
Part of the way, at least,
And their friends or lovers flew out a kind of skylight
Cut for loading hay.
I don't know, exactly, what happened then.
Except my sister moved to Switzerland.
My brother got a job
With Colgate-Palmolive.
He was selling soap in Lodi, California.
Later, in his car, & dressed
To die, or live again, forever,
I drove to my own, first wedding.
I smelled the stale boutonniere in my lapel,
A deceased young flower.
I wondered how my brother's Buick
Could go so fast, &,
Still questioning, or catching, a last time,
An old chill from childhood,
I thought: why me, why her, & knew it wouldn't last.

Though His Name Is Infinite, My Father Is Asleep

When my father disappeared,
He did not go into hiding.
In old age, he was infinite,
So where could he hide? No,
He went into his name,
He went into his name, & into
The way two words keep house,
Each syllable swept clean
Again when you say them;
That's how my father left,
And that's how my father went
Out of his house, forever.
Imagine a house without words,
The family speechless for once
At the kitchen table, & all night
A hard wind ruining
The mottled skin of plums
In the orchard, & no one
Lifting a finger to stop it.
But imagine no word for "house,"
Or wind in a bare place always,
And soon it will all disappear—
Brick, & stone, & wood—all three
Are wind when you can't say
"House," & know, anymore, what it is.
Say Father, then, to no one,
Or say my father was, himself,
A house, or say each word's a house,
Some lit & some abandoned.
Then go one step further,
And say a name is a home,
As remote & as intimate.
Say *home*, then, or say, "I'll
Never go home again," or say,

Years later, with that baffled,
Ironic smile, "I'm on my way
Home," or say, as he did not,
"I'm going into my name."
Go further; take a chance, & say
A name is intimate. Repeat all
The names you know, all
The names you've ever heard,
The living & the dead, the precise
Light snow of their syllables.
Say your own name, or say
A last name, say mine, say his,
Say a name so old & frayed
By common use it's lost
All meaning now, & sounds
Like a house being swept out,
Like wind where there's no house.
Say finally there is no way
To document this, or describe
The passing of a father, that
Faint scent of time, or how
He swore delicately, quickly
Against it without ever appearing
To hurry the ceremony of swearing.
And say, too, how you disliked
And loved him, how he stays up
All night now in two words,
How his worn out, infinite name
Outwits death when you say it.
And say finally how the things
He had to do for you
Humiliated him until
He could not get his breath, & say
How much they mattered, how
Necessary he was. And then,
Before sleep, admit, also,
That his name is nothing,
Light as three syllables,

Lighter than pain or art, lighter
Than history, & tell how two words,
That mean nothing to anyone
Else, once meant a world
To you; how sometimes, even you,
In the sweep of those syllables,
Wind, crushed bone, & ashes—
Begin to live again.

I lay my head sideways on the desk,
My fingers interlocked under my cheekbones,
My eyes closed. It was a three-room schoolhouse,
White, with a small bell tower, an oak tree.
From where I sat, on still days, I'd watch
The oak, the prisoner of that sky, or read
The desk carved with adults' names: Marietta
Martin, Truman Finnell, Marjorie Elm;
The wood hacked or lovingly hollowed, the flies
Settling on the obsolete & built-in inkwells.
I remember, tonight, only details, how
Mrs. Avery, now gone, was standing then
In her beige dress, its quiet, gazelle print
Still dark with lines of perspiration from
The day before; how Gracie Chin had just
Shown me how to draw, with chalk, a Chinese
Ideogram. Where did she go, white thigh
With one still freckle, lost in silk?
No one would say for sure, so that I'd know,
So that all shapes, for days after, seemed
Brushstrokes in Chinese: countries on maps
That shifted, changed colors, or disappeared:
Lithuania, Prussia, Bessarabia;
The numbers four & seven; the question mark.
That year, I ate almost nothing.
I thought my parents weren't my real parents,
I thought there'd been some terrible mistake.
At recess I would sit alone, seeing
In the print of each leaf shadow, an ideogram—
Still, indecipherable, beneath the green sound
The bell still made, even after it had faded,
When the dust-covered leaves of the oak tree
Quivered, slightly, if I looked up in time.
And my father, so distant in those days,

Where did he go, that autumn, when he chose
The chaste, faint ideogram of ash, & I had
To leave him there, white bones in a puzzle
By a plum tree, the sun rising over
The Sierras? It is not Chinese, but English—
When the past tense, when you first learn to use it
As a child, throws all the verbs in the language
Into the long, flat shade of houses you
Ride past, & into town. Your father's driving.
On winter evenings, the lights would come on earlier.
People would be shopping for Christmas. Each hand,
With one whorl of its fingerprints, with twenty
Delicate bones inside it, reaching up
To touch some bolt of cloth, or choose a gift,
A little different from any other hand.
You know how the past tense turns a sentence dark,
But leaves names, lovers, places showing through:
Gracie Chin, my father, Lithuania;
A beige dress where dark gazelles hold still?
Outside, it's snowing, cold, & a New Year.
The trees & streets are turning white.
I always thought he would come back like this.
I always thought he wouldn't dare be seen.

The last thing my father did for me
Was map a way: he died, & so
Made death possible. If he could do it, I
Will also, someday, be so honored. Once,

At night, I walked through the lit streets
Of New York, from the Gramercy Park Hotel
Up Lexington & at that hour, alone,
I stopped hearing traffic, voices, the racket

Of spring wind lifting a newspaper high
Above the lights. The streets wet,
And shining. No sounds. Once,

When I saw my son be born, I thought
How loud this world must be to him, how final.

That night, out of respect for someone missing,
I stopped listening to it.

Out of respect for someone missing,
I have to say

This isn't the whole story.
The fact is, I was still in love.
My father died, & I was still in love. I know
It's in bad taste to say it quite this way. Tell me,
How *would* you say it?

The story goes: wanting to be alone & wanting
The easy loneliness of travelers,

I said good-bye in an airport & flew west.
It happened otherwise.
And where I'd held her close to me,
My skin felt raw, & flayed.

Descending, I looked down at light lacquering fields
Of pale vines, & small towns, each
With a water tower; then the shadows of wings;
Then nothing.

My only advice is not to go away.
Or, go away. Most

Of my decisions have been wrong.

When I wake, I lift cold water
To my face. I close my eyes.

A body wishes to be held, & held, & what
Can you do about that?

Because there are faces I might never see again,
There are two things I want to remember
About light, & what it does to us.

Her bright, green eyes at an airport—how they widened
As if in disbelief;
And my father opening the gate: a lit, & silent

City.

Whenever I listen to Billie Holiday, I am reminded
That I, too, was once banished from New York City.
Not because of drugs or because I was interesting enough
For any wan, overworked patrolman to worry about—
His expression usually a great, gauzy spiderweb of bewilderment
Over his face—I was banished from New York City by a woman.
Sometimes, after we had stopped laughing, I would look
At her & see a cold note of sorrow or puzzlement go
Over her face as if someone else were there, behind it,
Not laughing at all. We were, I think, "in love." No, I'm sure.
If my house burned down tomorrow morning, & if I & my wife
And son stood looking on at the flames, & if, then,
Someone stepped out of the crowd of bystanders
And said to me: "Didn't you once know . . . ?" *No.* But if
One of the flames, rising up in the scherzo of fire, turned
All the windows blank with light, & if that flame could speak,
And if it said to me: "You loved her, didn't you?" I'd answer,
Hands in my pockets, "Yes." And then I'd let fire & misfortune
Overwhelm my life. Sometimes, remembering those days,
I watch a warm, dry wind bothering a whole line of elms
And maples along a street in this neighborhood until
They're all moving at once, until I feel just like them,
Trembling & in unison. None of this matters now,
But I never felt alone all that year, & if I had sorrows,
I also had laughter, the affliction of angels & children.
Which can set a whole house on fire if you'd let it. And even then
You might still laugh to see all of your belongings set you free
In one long choiring of flames that sang only to you—
Either because no one else could hear them, or because
No one else wanted to. And, mostly, because they know.
They know such music cannot last, & that it would
Tear them apart if they listened. In those days,
I was, in fact, already married, just as I am now,
Although to another woman. And that day I could have stayed

In New York. I had friends there. I could have strayed
Up Lexington Avenue, or down to Third, & caught a faint
Glistening of the sea between the buildings. But all I wanted
Was to hold her all morning, until her body was, again,
A bright field, or until we both reached some thicket
As if at the end of a lane, or at the end of all desire,
And where we could, therefore, be alone again, & make
Some dignity out of loneliness. As, mostly, people cannot do.
Billie Holiday, whose life was shorter & more humiliating
Than my own, would have understood all this, if only
Because even in her late addiction & her bloodstream's
Hallelujahs, she, too, sang often of some affair, or someone
Gone, & therefore permanent. And sometimes she sang for
Nothing, even then, & it isn't anyone's business, if she did.
That morning, when *she* asked me to leave, wearing only
The apricot tinted, fraying chemise, I wanted to stay.
But I also wanted to go, to lose her suddenly, almost
For no reason, & certainly without any explanation.
I remember looking down at a pair of singular tracks
Made in a light snow the night before, at how they were
Gradually effacing themselves beneath the tires
Of the morning traffic, & thinking that my only other choice
Was fire, ashes, abandonment, solitude. All of which happened
Anyway, & soon after, & by divorce. I know this isn't much.
But I wanted to explain this life to you, even if
I had to become, over the years, someone else to do it.
You have to think of me what you think of me. I had
To live my life, even its late, florid style. Before
You judge this, think of her. Then think of fire,
Its laughter, the music of splintering beams & glass,
The flames reaching through the second story of a house
Almost as if to—mistakenly—rescue someone who
Left you years ago. It is so American, fire. So like us.
Its desolation. And its eventual, brief triumph.

Tonight, holding a stranger in my arms—
Suddenly a downpour, a late
Summer storm. I thought of you, alone or
Not alone in that distant city,
And at that hour when the punk musicians' bars,
And the carpeted bars,
With their well-coiffed, careful clientele,
Are closing—
Those strangers pairing off at last & each desiring
What little mercy the other can
Afford. That
Wasted breath of neon light a frail
Tattoo or come-on in pools
Of rain. That street. That rain.
No. *Our* street. *Our* rain. Holding her, not you,
I watched it finally
Empty, watched until the streaked,
Reddening light of dawn came back & touched
The quiet brick of empty dance halls, touched,
Behind the blackened tavern windows, a girl's cast off
Blouse; touched even the pocked faces of musicians on
The posters there: *Gun Club; Millions
Of Dead Cops*—almost as if dawn light could
Hold all things, each piece
Of shattered glass, as if to somehow bless them,
Or make them whole again.
It can't, or won't.
And it is late for blessings: All night
I've held a woman who,
Tomorrow, I will not want to see again, & who,
Tomorrow, probably will feel the same
For me. And so at last the two of us
Will have something in common:
A slight embarrassment, or,

Someday in winter, passing on a street,
A quick, amused glance before
We turn away.
I don't expect much anymore; or else
That city is so far away by now it seems
Made of great light, & distance,
Even though it was, mostly, only a house
Like any other, lit at dinnertime
By human speech, the oldest of stories; something
In common. I remember now,
After scolding him,
The precise & careful way
My two-year-old son once offered me
The crust of his own bread, holding it out
So solemnly, as if it mattered, holding it
With great care.

𝓔 Whitman:

I say we had better look our nation searchingly
in the face, like a physician diagnosing some deep disease.
—Democratic Vistas

Look for me under your bootsoles.

On Long Island, they moved my clapboard house
Across a turnpike, & then felt so guilty they
Named a shopping center after me!

Now that I'm required reading in your high schools,
Teenagers call me a fool.
Now what I sang stops breathing.

And yet
It was only when everyone stopped believing in me
That I began to live again—
First in the thin whine of Montana fence wire,
Then in the transparent, cast-off garments hung
In the windows of the poorest families,
Then in the glad music of Charlie Parker.
At times now,
I even come back to watch you
From the eyes of a taciturn boy at Malibu.
Across the counter at the beach concession stand,
I sell you hot dogs, Pepsis, cigarettes—
My blond hair long, greasy, & swept back
In a vain old ducktail, deliciously
Out of style.
And no one notices.
Once, I even came back as *me,*
An aging homosexual who ran the Tilt-a-Whirl
At county fairs, the chilled paint on each gondola
Changing color as it picked up speed,

And a Mardi Gras tattoo on my left shoulder.
A few of you must have seen my photographs,
For when you looked back,
I thought you caught the meaning of my stare:

Still water,
Merciless.

A Kosmos. One of the roughs.

And Charlie Parker's grave outside Kansas City
Covered with weeds.

Leave me alone.
A father who's outlived his only child.

To find me now will cost you everything.

I don't know what happens to grass.
But it doesn't die, exactly.
It turns white, in winter, but stays there,
A few yards from the ditch,
Then comes back in March,
Turning a green that has nothing
To do with us.
Mostly, it's just yellow, or tan.
It blends in,
Swayed by the wind, maybe, but not by any emotion,
Or partisan stripe.
You can misread it, at times:
I have seen it almost appear
To fight long & well
For its right to be, & be grass, when
I tried pulling it out.
I thought I could almost sense it digging in,
Not with reproach, exactly,
But with a kind of rare tact that I miss,
Sometimes, in others.
And besides, if you really wanted it out,
You'd have to disc it under,
Standing on a shuddering Case tractor,
And staring into the distance like
Somebody with a vision
In the wrong place for visions.
With time, you'd feel silly.
And, always, it comes back:
At the end of some winter when
The sky has neither sun, nor snow,
Nor anything personal,
You'd be wary of any impulse
That seemed mostly cosmetic.
It's all a matter of taste,

And how taste changes.
Besides, in March, the fields are wet;
The trucks & machinery won't start,
And the blades of the disc won't turn,
Usually, because of the rust.
That's when you notice the grass coming back,
In some other spot, & with a different look
This time, as if it had an idea
For a peninsula, maybe, or its shape
Reclining on a map you almost
Begin to remember.
In March, my father spent hours
Just piecing together some puzzle
That might start up a tractor,
Or set the tines of a cultivator
Or spring tooth right,
And do it without paying money.
Those rows of gray earth that look "combed,"
Between each row of vines,
And run off to the horizon
As you drive past?
You could almost say
It was almost pretty.
But this place isn't France.
For years, they've made only raisins,
And a cheap, sweet wine.
And someone had to work late,
As bored as you are, probably,
But with the added headache of
Owning some piece of land
That never gave up much
Without a mute argument.
The lucky sold out to subdividers,
But this is for one who stayed,
And how, after a few years,
He even felt sympathy for grass—
Then felt *that* turn into a resentment
Which grew, finally, into

A variety of puzzled envy:
Turning a little grass under
With each acre,
And turning it under for miles,
While half his life, spent
On top of a tractor,
Went by, unnoticed, without feast days
Or celebrations—opening his mailbox
At the roadside which was incapable
Of looking any different—
More picturesque, or less common—
The rank but still blossoming weeds
Stirring a little, maybe,
As you drove past,
But then growing still again.

Two Variations on a Theme by Kobayashi

The year I returned to my village, the papers
And the mail, uncensored, were delivered
Faithfully, each day.
They treated me with kindness
Where I worked, & the bars, softly lighted,
Opened every night with their music.
Appointed Master of Riddles,
I felt I had stepped onto the dock of the New World,
Toting the old one (a fresh book of poems!)
On my back. Even strangers
Bought me drinks, & someone assured me that
I would be able to get any drug I wanted,
Should I desire drugs.
And when I drove to Arkansas to read
My poems, & saw the Ozarks—
Hills full of shifting, tethered mists & a flower
That turned whole meadows white
Against the anxious hint of leaves—& when
Some of my audience walked out because I read a poem
With two obscene words, I was delighted!
For in the North, obscenities are quaint.
That year, I taught one child how to hear
Hexameters in English, & she
Stopped crying about things she could do
Nothing to change. That year,
Because I play no instrument, I met
Many musicians—they spoke to me, mostly,
Of poetry, & I told them
How, if one doesn't have much time, rhyme
And a strong refrain line ought to
Govern everything—especially if one finds himself
In a republic determined to stay young
At any cost. Something new,
I reminded them, would come, even from their fatigue

After closing. Twice, my son
Came to visit me.
And I showed him two caves in Missouri.
Mark Twain, as a child, had played in one of them.
The cave, our tour guide said, was
Over one hundred million years old. My son
Loved it—even though it is lighted
Now, throughout, & I kept wishing that the cave
Were darker, or that I was younger.
There was nothing I could do
About either, & the blonde girl
Showing it to us knew all her lines
"By heart." Almost pretty, but she looked as if
Nothing in the world could make her laugh.
She & her children will, I'm sure, inherit this earth.

My son is four, & curious.
That year, I had to explain
My father's death to him, & also
The idea of heaven, & how
One got there, physically, after death. Therefore,
I had to lie for the first time
To my son, & therefore I had to give him up
A little more.
And though my wife & I spoke of reconciliation,
The snows came down with their ancient,
Cruel jokes, & each one
Was just as funny. Just as cruel.
We both felt stronger, after hearing
Them, & I went on
Living in my decaying neighborhood with the finch,
The elm, the spider, & the mouse,
And, if they could speak,
Each one spoke to me of its lowly position,
Its pathetic marriage, its doomed romance, & how
Much it hated the village—
And each one had different problems, different desires!
That year, the moon looked, each dawn,

Like a jilted suitor, a boy with an ashen face,
Sitting alone in the pool hall.
My neighbors & the townspeople avoided me,
But with the respect or courtesy
One shows for something
Misunderstood, passing, perhaps dangerous
To the education of their children—
But still a fact, like the woods sloping down
Behind an abandoned row of houses
Condemned by the new highway commissioner: bird calls,
The gray smoke of a tramp's fire,
A place where the fox we surprised, once, moved
Too quickly for human description,
And too quietly.

                    ". . . No,
That year, I wore black,
And a headband flecked with crimson & meant
To terrify anyone in a gang of youths
I met, often, on the road. That year, because
Of the taxes required by the Shogunite, no one
Had any money, & often
I would pause, wondering how those who truly
Had something to complain of could
Bear it any longer—
Those who were poor & with sick children, whose father
Pawned heirlooms meant to last a thousand years—
The cold wind swirling through each split
Matting of rushes meant to hold
Their houses together,
Their frail argument against the wind,
Their kneeling to pray in a season
Of high fever.
I do not wish to exhibit a feeling which some,
Perhaps out of political ambition
Or simple indifference,

Might consider too generous & boastful.
Many of us thought the same things,
Many of us, in our youth, had known
Such people, & have indeed wondered where
They have gone.
Towed up the river to some new town,
We would look back at them as they
Waved to us from the pier.
We thought we would live forever, then;
We did not know we were lights dancing
On black water. Soon,
We stopped writing them long letters, although
Once, we would have said
Such letters continued to be written, always,
In our hearts. But it is
No longer fashionable to say such things, the way
We once said them, before we found out
About style, & how completely
It explains us to each other.
It is as if, without knowing it, we all
Suddenly longed to be diminished: lights going out
Along a river, & a whole
Town abandoned! But sometimes,
I still think of that great dead lord,
Whom I defended, &
For whom I would slit an enemy open, from
Forehead to abdomen, when he at last
Displayed that hint of hesitation
In the body, by which
One recognizes a liar. I moved, using one stroke;
No second thoughts.
It would have been the same for him
If I had discovered, in a sudden weightlessness
In my shoulders, a laughter throughout my whole body,
The same lie in myself.
                              "I know
There are those who think we are thieves
Interested only in profit.

I prefer to believe, with my old master,
That there are men & women in this world
For whom I would willingly give my life, &
That we, who studied in such schools,
Are the last to know
How to move gracefully
In those exact measures meant to correct
Time, which knows
Nothing of itself, nothing
Of the damage it can do,
And which it is condemned to do:
My wife is dead;
My daughter is beautiful;
The first snow has just fallen & if I am older
It is because I have looked out & noticed it.
It is because
It has tricked me into this final maneuver,
This turning toward a white window,
Something my master always told me it would do, &
Against which all swords are useless!"

There are places where the eye can starve,
But not here. Here, for example, is
The Piazza Navona, & here is his narrow room
Overlooking the Steps & the crowds of sunbathing
Tourists. And here is the Protestant Cemetery
Where Keats & Joseph Severn join hands
Forever under a little shawl of grass
And where Keats's name isn't even on
His gravestone, because it is on Severn's,
And Joseph Severn's infant son is buried
Two modest, grassy steps behind them both.
But you'd have to know the story—how bedridden
Keats wanted the inscription to be
Simple, & unbearable: "Here lies one
Whose name is writ in water." On a warm day,
I stood here with my two oldest friends.
I thought, then, that the three of us would be
Indissoluble at the end, & also that
We would all die, of course. And not die.
And maybe we should have joined hands at that
Moment. We didn't. All we did was follow
A lame man in a rumpled suit who climbed
A slight incline of graves blurring into
The passing marble of other graves to visit
The vacant home of whatever is not left
Of Shelley & Trelawney. That walk uphill must
Be hard if you can't walk. At the top, the man
Wheezed for breath; sweat beaded his face,
And his wife wore a look of concern so
Habitual it seemed more like the way
Our bodies, someday, will have to wear stone.
Later that night, the three of us strolled,
Our arms around each other, through the Via
Del Corso & toward the Piazza di Espagna

As each street grew quieter until
Finally we heard nothing at the end
Except the occasional scrape of our own steps,
And so said good-bye. Among such friends,
Who never allowed anything, still alive,
To die, I'd almost forgotten that what
Most people leave behind them disappears.
Three days later, staying alone in a cheap
Hotel in Naples, I noticed a child's smeared
Fingerprint on a bannister. It
Had been indifferently preserved beneath
A patina of varnish applied, I guessed, after
The last war. It seemed I could almost hear
His shout, years later, on that street. But this
Is speculation, & no doubt the simplest fact
Could shame me. Perhaps the child was from
Calabria, & went back to it with
A mother who failed to find work, & perhaps
The child died there, twenty years ago,
Of malaria. It was so common then—
The children crying to the doctors for quinine.
And to the tourists, who looked like doctors, for quinine.
It was so common you did not expect an aria,
And not much on a gravestone, either—although
His name is on it, & weathered stone still wears
His name—not the way a girl might wear
The too large, faded blue workshirt of
A lover as she walks thoughtfully through
The Via Fratelli to buy bread, shrimp,
And wine for the evening meal with candles &
The laughter of her friends, & later the sweet
Enkindling of desire; but something else, something
Cut simply in stone by hand & meant to last
Because of the way a name, any name,
Is empty. And not empty. And almost enough.

In the background, a few shacks & overturned carts
And a gray sky holding the singular pallor of Lent.
And here the crowd of onlookers, though a few of them
Must be intimate with the victim,
Have been advised to keep their distance.
The young man walking alone in handcuffs that join
Each wrist in something that is not prayer, although
It is as urgent, wears
A brown tweed coat flecked with white, a white shirt
Open at the collar.
And beside him, the broad, curving tracks of a bus that
Passed earlier through the thawing mud . . . they seem
To lead him out of the photograph & toward
What I imagine is
The firing squad: a few distant cousins & neighbors
Assembled by order of the State—beside
The wall of a closed schoolhouse.
Two of the men uneasily holding rifles, a barber
And an unemployed postal clerk,
Are thinking of nothing except perhaps the first snowfall
Last year in the village, how it covered & simplified
Everything—the ruts in the road & the distant
Stubble in the fields—& of how they cannot be,
Now, any part of that. Still,
They understand well enough why
The man murdered the girl's uncle with an axe,
Just as they know why his language,
Because it was not official & had to be translated
Into Czech at the trial, failed to convince
Anyone of its passion. And if
The red-faced uncle kept threatening the girl
Until she at last succumbed under a browning hedge, & if
The young man had to use three strokes with the axe
To finish the job—well, they shrug,

All he had, that day, was an axe.
And besides, the barber & the clerk suspect that this boy,
Whom they have known for half their lives,
Had really intended to kill the girl that evening—
Never the uncle.
In a lost culture of fortune tellers, unemployable
Horse traders, & a frank beauty the world
Will not allow,
It was the time of such things, it was late summer,
And it is time now, the two executioners agree,
That all of this ended. This is
Jarabina. 1963. And if
Koudelka tells us nothing else about this scene,
I think he is right, if only because
The young man walks outside time now, & is not
So much a murderer as he is, simply, a man
About to be executed by his neighbors. . . .
And so it is important to all of them that he behave
With a certain tact & dignity as he walks
Of his own accord but with shoulders hunched,
Up to the wall of the empty schoolhouse;
And, turning his head
First to one side, then to the other,
He lets them slip the blindfold over his eyes
And secure it with an old gentleness
They have shared
Since birth. And perhaps at this moment
All three of them remember slipping light scarves,
Fashioned into halters,
Over the muzzles of horses, & the quickness of horses.
And if the boy has forgiven them in advance
By such a slight gesture, this turning of his head,
It is because he knows, as they do, too,
Not only that terror is a state
Of complete understanding, but also that
In a few years, this whole village, with its cockeyed
Shacks, tea leaves, promiscuity between cousins,
Idle horse thieves, & pale lilacs used

To cure the insane,
Will be gone—bulldozed away so that the land
Will lie black & fallow & without history.
And nothing will be planted there, or buried,
As the same flocks of sparrows
Will go on gathering, each spring, in the high dark
Of these trees.
Still, it is impossible not to see
That the young man has washed & combed his hair
For this last day on earth; it is impossible
Not to see how one of the policemen has turned back
To the crowd as if to prevent
Any mother or sister from rushing forward—
Although neither one, if she is here, seems
About to move. And in the background,
You can see that a few of the houses are entirely white,
Like a snowfall persisting into spring,
Or into oblivion, though this
May be the fault of the photograph or its development
Under such circumstances. . . .
And now even the children in the crowd, who have gathered
To watch all this, appear to be growing bored
With the procedures & the waiting.
I suppose that the young man's face,
Without looking up, spoke silently to Koudelka as he passed,
Just as it speaks now, to me, from this photograph.
Now that there is nothing either of us can do for him.
His hair is clean & washed, & his coat is buttoned.
Except for his handcuffs, he looks as if
He is beginning a long journey, or going out,
For the first time into the world. . . .
He must have thought he could get away with this,
Or else he must have thought he loved her.
It is too late to inquire.
It is mid-afternoon & twenty years too late,
And even the language he used to explain it all
Is dying a little more, each moment, as I write this—
And as I begin to realize that

This ancient, still blossoming English
Will also begin to die, someday, to crack & collapse
Under its own weight—
Though that will not happen for years & years,
And long after the barber & the clerk
Have lowered their rifles & turned away to vomit
For what seems like a long time, & then,
Because there is nothing else for them to do,
They will walk home together, talking softly in a language
That has never been written down.
If you look closely at the two of them
Sweating in their black wool suits,
You can see how even their daily behavior,
The way they avoid the subject,
Has become an art:
One talks of his daughter, who is learning to dance.
The other mentions his mother, who died, last year—
When the orchards were simple with their fruit,
And ripe—of an undiagnosed illness.
And if the lots they pass are empty because the horses
Were shipped off years ago to Warsaw
For the meat on their backs?
And if there is no hope for this,
Or any poetry?
On their lips the quick syllables of their
Language fly & darken into a few, last
Delicious phrases, arpeggios—
Even though they are talking of ordinary life
As they pass the smells of cooking
Which rise in smoke from the poorest of houses
And even from stoves carried outdoors & burning,
As fuel, the cheap paneling of shacks
Which the government gave them.
Until it seems that all they are
Rises in smoke,
As it always has,
And as it will continue to do in this place
For a few more years.

In Josef Koudelka's photograph, untitled & with no date
Given to help us with history, a man wearing
Dark clothes is squatting, his right hand raised slightly,
As if in explanation, & because he is talking,
Seriously now, to a horse that would be white except
For its markings—the darkness around its eyes, muzzle,
Legs & tail, by which it is, technically, a gray, or a dapple gray,
With a streak of pure white like heavy cream on its rump.
There is a wall behind them both, which, like most walls, has
No ideas, & nothing to make us feel comfortable. . . .
After a while, because I know so little, &
Because the muted sunlight on that wall will not change,
I begin to believe that the man's wife & children
Were shot & thrown into a ditch a week before this picture
Was taken, that this is still Czechoslovakia, & that there is
The beginning of spring in the air. That is why
The man is talking, & as clearly as he can, to a horse.
He is trying to explain these things,
While the horse, gray as those days at the end
Of winter, when days seem lost in thought, is, after all,
Only a horse. No doubt the man knows people he could talk to:
The bars are open by now, but he has chosen
To confide in this gelding, as he once did to his own small
Children, who could not, finally, understand him any better.
This afternoon, in the middle of his life & in the middle
Of this war, a man is trying to stay sane.
To stay sane he must keep talking to a horse, its blinders
On & a rough snaffle bit still in its mouth, wearing
Away the corners of its mouth, with one ear cocked forward to listen,
While the other ear tilts backward slightly, inattentive,
As if suddenly catching a music behind it. Of course,
I have to admit I have made all of this up, & that
It could be wrong to make up anything. Perhaps the man is perfectly
Happy. Perhaps Koudelka arranged all of this

And then took the picture as a way of saying
Good-bye to everyone who saw it, & perhaps Josef Koudelka was
Only two years old when the Nazis invaded Prague.
I do not wish to interfere, Reader, with your solitude—
So different from my own. In fact, I would take back everything
I've said here, if that would make you feel any better,
Unless even that retraction would amount to a milder way
Of interfering; & a way by which you might suspect me
Of some subtlety. Or mistake me for someone else, someone
Not disinterested enough in what you might think
Of this. Of the photograph. Of me.
Once, I was in love with a woman, & when I looked at her
My face altered & took on the shape of her face,
Made thin by alcohol, sorrowing, brave. And though
There was a kind of pain in her face, I felt no pain
When this happened to mine, when the bones
Of my own face seemed to change. But even this
Did not do us any good, &, one day,
She went mad, waking in tears she mistook for blood,
And feeling little else except for this concern about bleeding
Without pain. I drove her to the hospital, & then,
After a few days, she told me she had another lover. . . . So,
Walking up the street where it had been raining earlier,
Past the darkening glass of each shop window to the hotel,
I felt a sensation of peace flood my body, as if to cleanse it,
And thought it was because I had been told the truth. . . .
    But, you see,
Even that happiness became a lie, & even that was taken
From me, finally, as all lies are. . . . Later,
I realized that maybe I felt strong that night only
Because she was sick, for other reasons, & in that place.
And so began my long convalescence, & simple adulthood.
I never felt that way again, when I looked at anyone else;
I never felt my face change into any other face.
It is a difficult thing to do, & so maybe
It is just as well. That man, for instance. He was a *saboteur.*
He ended up talking to a horse, & hearing, on the street

Outside that alley, the Nazis celebrating, singing, even.
If he went mad beside that wall, I think his last question
Was whether they shot his wife & children before they threw them
Into the ditch, or after. For some reason, it mattered once,
If only to him. And before he turned into paper.

The Widening Spell
of the Leaves

Her husband left her suddenly. Then it was autumn.
And in those first, crisp days of a new life,
Each morning she would watch her son, a boy of seven,
Yawn before mounting the steps, glinting like a sea,
When the doors of the school bus opened.
And then she would dress, leaving the back way,
And hearing or overhearing the screen door close
Behind her, always the same, indifferent swish.
At that hour the frost on the lawn still held
Whorled fingerprints of cold, as if the cold had slept
There. Then she would climb in, she told me,
On the wrong side of the small, open car,
And sit quite still, an unlit cigarette in her hand,
And wait for him to come out and drive her
To work, as always. The first two times it happened
She was frightened, she said, because, waiting for him,
Something went wrong with Time. Later, she couldn't
Say whether an hour or only a few minutes
Had passed before she realized she didn't
Have a husband. Then she would lift herself
Awkwardly over the brake & gearshift, spilling
Gently backward into the driver's seat,
Her legs still on the wrong side a moment,
In mottled sunlight. For a second I almost glimpse
Her knees, slender & raised slightly like
A lover's. I know it's wrong to stare at them.
At this moment she is all alone; at this moment,
Because her mistake is so pathetic, she's crying.

Then she stops waiting. The car pulls out of the drive
And onto the street each day. The weeks pass, & then
The months; then the years are blending into
Tables set for two, & even anger dies.
On Sundays, hiking, the boy finds wildflowers.

They look them up in a field guide before
She places them, like stillness itself, in a vase—
Cloisonné, its gray background lustrous, lacquered.
There is a line both of them know by heart,
And the boy repeats it idly, a sentence composed
In madness while its poet sat, as still
As any flower in his cell, hearing beyond it
The cries of the asylum, & beyond that, nothing.
Nothing, though the carriages of London keep
Whispering through its hushed streets forever,
Past the silently clinging chimney sweep
In the mild drizzle of 1756;
And the poet, alone with his holy cat, watches
A dung beetle, "Whose sight is precious to God,"
Scurry across wet stone, while the boy is chanting:
"The Right Names for Flowers Are Hush'd in Heaven."
"'Still in Heaven. . . .' Christopher Smart," she adds.
She adds half a bay leaf to the simmering stew.

But when I think of her, nothing has happened yet.
It is this moment before she remembers
Her husband isn't there, the moment before
The Indian summers of her bare legs appear,
Then disappear, the week before the maples'
Yellowing leaves lining her street all turn
To the colors of horses: roans, sorrels, duns,
Chestnuts, bays, blacks, then a final
Liver-white quilt of Appaloosa
Unraveling over the first, brief snow.
Then the zebra shades & short days of winter.
When I think of her, she's still sitting there,
On the wrong side of the car, intent, staring,
As her thought collects in pools yet keeps
Widening until, now, it casts its spell—
And then the scene is one of great stillness ripening,
Enlarging, spreading to include the boy who sits
Like stillness itself above the graffiti carved
Into his desk by students who are older now,

And wilder. It is five minutes into his morning recess,
And the boy will not go out. He sits alone,
Listening, the classroom windowless—& he knows
The moment when the stillness finds his father
With his shoulders stooped, unmoving, in another state.
The father simply stands there now, a teapot whistling
In the cramped kitchen of his studio; he gazes
Straight ahead into what seems to him a valley
Filling with snow until the end of time.
He's seeing things. In front of him there's only
A white cupboard, some dishes, an ashtray displaying
The name of a casino. But the woman won't relent:
The spell's hush is on the boy's pencil in its tray;
It's on the desk & dry leaves pinned to the walls. . . .
The boy listens, & does not listen, both hears
And does not hear the older students, those
Already in junior high, lounging outside
In the corridor, acknowledging each other—
Their whispers are the high, light rustling of leaves
Above the vagrant he passes on the way home,
The one intent on sleeping this world away,
A first chill entering the park as he shoves
His chapped hands deeper between his knees—
The boy watches this as if in the sleep of the other. . . .
And all of this three years before the father
Hears a secret club of voices, steps onto an ark
Of stories, floating, three times each week,
Past him, through him, admitting its powerlessness,
And God. Forgive me, I keep watching them now,
In this moment two days after the father has slumped out,
I keep waiting for the next thing to happen,
And that is the problem: nothing happens, nothing
Happens at all. It is as if Time Itself
Sticks without knowing it in this wide place
I had mistaken for a moment, sticks
Like the tip of the father's left forefinger
To the unwiped, greasy, kitchen countertop.

1.

Even when we finally had to burn them, the gray, stately
Trunks of malagas, the tough, already yellowing limbs
Of muscats—acres of them in those years, hacked, stacked
In piles, then doused with kerosene—even their fires
Flaring all night in what were suddenly bare fields—
Looked older than the city dressed in its distant light.
Of course after the fires passed it was all for sale.
Some vacant lots were leased to milkweed & black-eyed Susans
For a few months; then pavement, billboards, the treeless yards,
And at the end of each street a sky that looked painted in.

What's gone is moon's silk; what's gone has rotted the circles from
    Luna Moth & Shasta Daisy.
Beyond the flies on the sills, beyond the stained glass with its sheep
Accumulating like curious tourists, you could hear the sound of
    hammering grow louder each week
In Leisure Villa & Sierra Madre. The walls of our ridiculous, rural parish,
Lined with poor reproductions of paintings meant to instruct us,
Seemed only a setting for the veiled women addicted to prayer.
What floats back now is the Virgin, a Mary holding out an apronful
    of bread,
A cold sea behind her & a distracted look on her face. I thought it meant
She was remembering a girlhood, the faint odor, garlic & mint, of a man
Asleep beside a tree-lined road. It was instructive, they said,
If it made you sad. It was a complete waste of time, & childhood, & so,
I suppose now it was instructive: the way the body woke alone,
The way the vineyards vanished into patterns of lime & yellow dolphins
Rising in pairs to the surface of a Formica countertop, the way
The sky began to take up residence in a few, cramped words

As I sat reading them there. The naked human body is the grave in blossom;
    it is both
Sad & instructive. And which withered cane from which withered vine
    of malagas
Would you choose to carry into Hell if you left now?

2.

for James Wright

Today, hearing the empty clang of a rope against
A flagpole, the children in school, the slow squeal of swings
In the playground, a day of rain & gusts
Of wind, I noticed the overleaf of his book—
How someone had tried hard to make
The illustration look like snow that had fallen in the shape
Of a horse; it looked, instead, like someone wrapped in bandages.
Someone alone & wrapped in bandages who could not see out,
Who would never be permitted to see out
As a gust of rain swept over the swimming pool, over
The thin walls of my apartment, twenty years ago.
If I look in the window I can see the book open on the counter;
I am reading it there; I am alone.
Everyone else in the world is in bed with someone else.
If they sleep, they sleep with a lock of the other's hair
In their lips, but the world is one short,
An odd number, & so God has given me a book of poems.
And suddenly the boy sitting there isn't funny anymore.
And in that moment the one
Wrapped in bandages wants only to look out once,
Even at a gust of rain blemishing the pool,
Even at a scuffed shoe passing.
Poor shoe, poor rain, poor sprawl of stucco & plywood.
And death, poorest of cousins, back turned
In all the photographs,
Wanting his mouth for a souvenir.

3.

In 1965, if anything was worth worshipping in that city,
It was in the old neighborhood rife with eucalyptus & a few,
    brooding mulberries,
It was the lioness asleep in the zoo, unmoved by the taunts
Of children or the trash they threw, sometimes on fire for a moment,
    into her cage.
It was the way she endured it: heat, rain, misfortune; turning on her
    heels always
Away from you as if there were two worlds, as if you were lost
In this one. She could have killed a man with one swipe
Of her paw, but she did not. And that is why, in the next world,
She has come back as a poem already written for her, & hidden
In this one. This one which fills us with longing. Which bores her.
In 1965 in that city, no one knew less than a boy of nineteen, still a virgin,
Still brimming over with extinct love;
His face shining with acne he'd rubbed raw with a hand towel
To make it disappear; instead, it blistered, & later,
Looking in the mirror, he thought such blisters might be
The visible evidence of the soul. Laugh, if you want to;
After all, the next world is a lioness & she moves without history,
    like a lioness,
And without mistakes. Besides, it's twenty years later.
By now that boy's already poured his first drink of the evening;
So have you, & no tense is as sad as the future's.
If I'm not laughing with you it's because I'm talking to myself again:

It should be one of those nights when you were wise & singular after
The rush & an almost virginal swirling in the veins;
Outside the motel on the outskirts, I waited.
And later I glanced out at the passing cypresses festooned in spiderwebs,
    or ice, & I drove.
The night you disappeared into the wholesale dark—whiskey & a cold wind
    & never coming home—
I sat reading in the steadfast lamplight; the story darkened,

And when you wouldn't come back,
I watched the autumn light fall across a photograph.
I watched the world take off its dress;
I saw the world's gooseflesh.
Later I saw you laughing with the others in the garden;
There was the smell of someone's cigarette,
And then the smell of crushed gravel on a driveway after a rain.

Once, there was a kind of beauty, like a sail.
It was white, like a sail, & . . .
Once under way, you could watch even the people you worked with
    grow distant, until they seemed perfectly composed,
The way a shoreline falls into place behind you. The way it appears so
    untroubled when you are at sea.
At sea I woke in chills, I shivered in the wake of your pleasure.
They will say all this is sad & instructive, but it isn't.
Nor is there any scent of grief in such a story.

And afterward only the ordinary, slowly closing white ocean of the arm—
    something to witness—
Because it is not a miracle to be here, sweeping up before dawn, &
    because these windowsills
Do not open onto a New World but only onto the flat dark gleaming
    of rails:
You can hear the scoring of steel on steel,
And through a boxcar's open door, you can see a matted swath of straw
    or snow for a moment in the first light;
And then the world in its one dress, the park drowsing in mist.
If only we could have held hands, as the straitjacketed mad appear to do!
But remember in that apartment twenty years ago, how—just by looking
    at it carefully—
It took nothing more than a scuffed shoe to get you high,
Or a dry leaf blown into a bedroom where you sat reading late at night,
Or the remembered, twisted shape of a yellowing vine you once threw—
    steaming suddenly in the first, warm sunlight—
Onto a pile for burning.
And later, staring into those fires, how the sleepless shape of each flame

Held your attention like someone's nakedness, a nakedness
The world clothes in light until it's a city. This city.
I leave you here, with the next world already beginning to stir, & you wide
   awake in this one.
This one with the first traffic beginning just beyond your doorstep in the
   slow gauze of dawn—
And the trees & hedges lining your street in the oldest neighborhood?
So thick now, so overgrown, they look as if they had always been there?
And the first frost?
Anything is enough if you know how poor you are.
You could step out now in wonder.

Slow Child with a Book of Birds

1.

The snow that has no name is just
This snow, falling so thick it seems
To pause a moment in midair.
When I had stared long enough at it, the word
That held it showed me only a swirling without
A name, a piece of untalkative sky intact
Above a row of houses, & blankness filling
The frames of every doorway, a white
That made the dark around it visible.

Yesterday, the slow child on the bus, talkative
Amidst the fully evolved quiet of those
Around us muffled in their parkas, was showing me
A Snowy Egret in the book he carried,
"No Regrets," he said, pointing to its eyes,
To a brassy, unassailable candor in them.
"No Regrets," he said again, for the pleasure
Of it, & smiled, absorbed in it,
The pages dog-eared, stained by crumbs, milk,
Snow, wonder, & his sweating hand.
No Regrets in his thin blue windbreaker
Disappearing into the swirling street,
And no one I saw the rest of that whole freezing
Overcast day remembered how to treat
The day as decently. Why was it
That the child's eyes in a flesh that held
The pallor of putty outshone all others then?
And why, in the rush-hour traffic, did he begin
To laugh out loud at something no one saw,
At the joke the falling snow was telling him?
Dodo look out where you're going I thought,
As a chorus of horns escorted him,

King of all the lifted, unrented dark
Of the office buildings that rose around us there,
Still smiling as he crossed against the light,
And then waving, with a studied
Formality, to each swearing, skidding driver,
The dark street turning slowly white.

2.

Is the Snowy Egret extinct by now?
Or does it only sound as if it is,
Or will be soon? Endangered like all else,
The dim name on the child's lips, a thin
Windbreaker all he has to show the blizzard
When it doesn't end?
When a species dims, what is the last
One left of it worth?
Is it priceless then, as a snow comes on?
A bird that afterward is just
Its name & illustration in a book,
A thing that would be worthless
Except for all the wealth within its
Name, & a plumage lost in the reproductions
Of it, the color on the pages always wrong,
The slightly off, off-white of its wings?
Isn't it wrong when a boy's so dumb
He keeps the world within him spinning
On less than most of us, on less than nothing,
On nothing but the wealthy names of birds
Extinct in a bird book he carries
Under a left arm tucked like a wing
To shield them, until the falling snow
Around him must be music? It must be,
For I say it is, and say so to a snow
Vanishing into a slate sea,
The snow Coleridge noticed even in
The heavy drifts of his habit, & who, nevertheless,
Would have inquired something of that slow child

Concerning flight, seeing his affliction as
A visitation also, in a way of seeing lost.
Isn't it wrong when a boy's so dumb
He has to watch the others for a sign
Of what to do, where to open the book
The teacher gives him? Coleridge at
The rail of a ship sailing back
From Malta—his mind surveying
Itself, the hushed, broken toys it carried
Home in a private ridicule & shame,
Watching as two sailors from America
Tortured a pelican on a deck by tossing
Scraps to it, then flailed it with sticks
When it tried to eat. . . . Coleridge
Saw the world to come.

3.

Once, in a spring thaw just before
Saigon fell to those who cared for it,
I walked the slowly warming banks
Of the Missouri bending at Rocheport.
In the current a thing of snow slipped by,
Unfrozen but warming,
Snow in a crusted altar gliding past,
A strutting crow its unhurrying priest,
Riding the carcass of something large.
In the frame houses that sailed
And lined the river's banks, overlooking it,
If every armchair wanted a doily on it,
And wanted Ice Capades on television,
And a bowl of Cheetos; if Lyle Pugh & his wife,
Garnette, joined hands to watch,
Then carcasses with crows will do for them
As well as stained glass & cathedrals.

In 1370, within earshot of Notre Dame,
These same crows (gathering wisely just

Out of range of a boy's 12-gauge
In the bare limbs of a tree) already
Had become adept at pecking out of the eyes
Of thieves lashed to their scaffolds
Lining the Seine. Villon admired them, such appetite!
And anything else refusing its own extinction.
He took his boots off on the bank,
And pared his nails with a knife,
A glinting that, disappearing,
Made Paris: beauty & murder.
If Villon had pitied the slow child,
This would not have prevented him
From lifting the kid's jacket and the strange
Bird book too, nor later, remembering him in his will,
From bequeathing him a mind and a knife to use it with.

4.

Lives in a book of extinct birds
Seem clearer than my own of drifted snow,
Of snow in drifts of other snows,
A gaunt, black motorcycle under me
As I drift up Emigration Canyon,
The shapes of the wind-driven snow,
Long curves that give up their shapes
To other shapes, curves like the shape
Of a woman laughing in bed, abandoned
To some foolish, endearing amusement,
Or a woman asleep, & drifts innumerable
And different, the miles becoming the way
She turned in that sleep, & the road
Winding up onto a canyon only
Unwinds again, coming to an end
In the fact of trash blown against
A storm fence on the interstate,
Sandwich wrappers from a picnic
And brown newspapers clinging to it,
While the boy with the bird book

Clutched in his arm smiles, for to him
It is all a music, a music
And a swirling in a world without an end.

5.

Of course there is another snow, the snow
In which the pages of all books turn to laughter,
And then into silence & a swirling, the snow
That begins with only a few flakes some afternoon,
And in an hour is a blizzard, the streets & houses
Disappearing from the world, & the world
A flying into itself that will not end
Until I believe, & confess believing, to
Swirls & darkness, that the world had dreamt
Itself, & left me in it so long unmolested
That I thought it real, & my life clutched tightly
As a bird book real also, though now it is all
One long flake by flake undreaming of itself
Until nothing is left of it but the counter
Of a diner, bowls of soup, the bent shoulders
Of warehouse workers where I recall a woman
Slipping her black tank top off without a word
To show me a waist, a snow without a name,
Who sang over & over in whispers the nonsense
Of "Wooly Bully" in my ear at some party
Twenty years ago, a summer of thick stars
Over us on a lawn, & oh the snow vanishing
Into the slate gray seas of blackboards.
The illustrations in a bird book open to
The tires passing over them, & the sky,
And oh the silent passengers on a bus
Who stared straight ahead at nothing, crows
And the disciples of crows, an arthritic hand
Clutching a Cheeto before the blaring set,
Oh & the whispering of snow forever in its
Undressing & undreaming, & oh the bright
Meaningless famine in her eyes—each species'—

Split-second puzzlement at what it is—
And oh oh the black & white of everything
Flooding the moment after, so wrong,
So certain of exactly what it is,
And not wrong: No Regrets, some food still stuck
Between his teeth in his off-white, foolish,
Endless grin, that unrelenting music
That makes all things a scattering & wheeling
Once again, the black seeds thrown out onto
The snow & window squealing shut just after—
The sudden, overcast quiet of the past tense.

The Perfection of Solitude: A Sequence

---

1. Oaxaca, 1983

And now the sunlight, gradually filling the lobby, strays over
The freckled hands of the desk clerk as he studies a racing form,
And strays, as it must have done so often, over the soiled,

Unbuttoned shirt of the porter, who smiles. Who smiles
Because there is something hopeless here, not only in this lobby
With the one stunted palm & cracked leather sofa, but here

In Oaxaca, in this moment when the plaza sleeps & is abandoned,
And the hunchback, still clutching his bowl & dream, turns in his sleep,
A solemn clack of billiards behind him. In this moment I sign my name

Onto the ledger of the Hotel França, & the vain, looping style
Of the signature, almost illegible, begins, in the long blossom & hush
Of its fade, to forget me: to look, somehow, already smaller, more distant

Than ever, dried & faded, as if no one is ever at home inside a name,
Or as if a name is only a scratch or sound enclosing some common
    abstinence:
The hush of the plaza & the empty tables outside the Café del Jardín, &,

Above them, tacked up on the green, closed shutters of the newsstand,
A poster for a boxing match in which the red & black stencilled letters are
Suddenly too clear, & too still. . . . I don't know why they are like this—

And the hush of the mountains above the slightly different hush
Of the plaza—but no, I see now it is the same hush, the hush that is
Held in paintings the way a breath is held, but held forever, & . . .

The closed shop fronts lining the Avenida Trujano, those smudged pastels
Of pink & blue that once must have celebrated the birth of children,
And an occasional, random mauve or yellow that celebrated nothing

Except mauve, or yellow; & two adolescent girls, some locks of their hair
Dyed vermilion in the lingering fashion of the time, who nap against
The recently whitewashed trunks of the high laurel trees there. . . . In

This moment, not one leaf is moving, & the cloud bank above it all
Does not move. And the woman who has been abandoned sleeps, & the wife
Of the governor sleeps. Actually, the moment I refer to happened
Years ago, & I remember gazing at the plaza the whole time so that
Nothing would change, so that nothing would ever change. . . . Five seconds

Later a bomb went off in the telegraph office & a young janitor who was

Sweeping up the place felt both his legs surprise him with their sudden
Absence. And later it was revealed that the people who made the bomb
Thought they were making a much smaller bomb, &, in fact, one of
    their group

Had been told to detain the janitor that day by any means possible, & so
The janitor, after sparring with his brother in a gym, was forced to throw
Their representative against the trunk of a taxi stalled in noon traffic

On the Calle de la Reforma, & later that day, watching the crowds filling
The plaza, I remembered talking over drinks on a lawn that swept down
Into a warm canal & a marsh speckled with shore birds, &, beyond that,

The mouth of the Connecticut River, &, beyond that, the sea. The guests
Who had gathered there, who seemed so completely what they wished
    to be,
Summer dresses, crisp chardonnay, were at leisure, & somehow in
    that leisure

You could feel a century beginning to come to an end. . . . I looked out,
    then,
Toward the sound, but there was nothing there except the usual pleasure
Boats, & whitecaps. And later, lying awake, the moon over that sea

So bright it lit the whole cabin, I remembered the time I made love once
To a woman in broad daylight in an empty classroom. Both of us were
Students then; we had been reading something. What was it? What it was,

Was a bright May morning, the day after Kent State. Both of us were
Married then, to others, & neither one of us especially wanted it
To happen. Like the children who skate endlessly in Auden's poem

About Brueghel, who didn't want to skate that long, then had to, at the edge
Of a pond, painted there, & no boy falling out of the sky above them.
The classroom was in the "lab school" of the university & was designed

For children, & wasn't going to be used for another day, although outside
We could hear students passing in the corridor, some of them calling
Out to each other, & some of them our friends who would try to close off,

In the next hour or so, the streets leading to the university, & then
The university. The idea was to form a sort of "human wall," & what was
Shocking, later, is how the media crews focused on the faces of women who

Had been beaten, who could not stop crying because of the simplicity
    of pain
At that moment. And suddenly she lifted off the dress she wore with one

Smooth, thoughtless gesture, & held it above her for a moment, & looked
    at me.

Any nakedness, the first time I saw it then, was still wonder. If we had
    looked
Away, through windows decorated for Easter, we could have seen the first
    busloads

Of police pulling onto the campus. And there was, afterward, the sharp tang
Of freedom mixing with loss, & mixing, somehow, with the paintings the
    children
Had made, which were all around us on those walls but dressed in their
    innocence

And encroaching upon the blackboard which held the slate, unencouraging
     hue
Of the Baltic Sea in winter. Or the sea that is always there, just beyond
The children who skated in the painting, & beyond the children who skated

There, when they painted; & what else is the thought of a child except

A kind of painting, I thought then. By then the woman was brushing
     her hair

In a small mirror she held. Years later, married again, lying awake
In that cabin, a sea & a moon & my son asleep in the next room near
     a piano—
Its ivory keys were so unreal in that light I thought they would wake him,

And quietly I went in to make sure he was still sleeping, & he was, although
I think now I went in just to see him there, & also because in a few hours
I would have to leave him forever, & because by that time I would need

To acquire the tact & decency to explain it all to him. And resist lying.

And sometimes later, walking in the crowd, I became the crowd.
     Which gift wraps

Its losses. Which listens to the tired spiel of compliments recited by a nude,
Teenage girl on display in a glass cage in Denver's porno district.
     There are
Two small holes drilled through the glass by which men can slip money
     through, &

The tips of her still budding nipples fit there. You can touch them
     & suck them
If you want to. The light overhead is like the fluorescent glare of a bus depot
As she keeps telling you how much she would like to fuck you, but can't,
     a wall

Of glass separating you from her. When she asks you to unzip, you don't,
   you
Apologize, & tell her she is beautiful, & she nods. Then you notice
   the tawny
Wrappings of a McDonald's cheeseburger behind her & think how
   someone probably

Had to bring it to her. Something about it reminds you of litter in a cage,
Of a zoo. As if she lives in a cage of glass. And then you imagine a pimp
In an outlandish paisley shirt, wide-brimmed hat, & bell bottoms
   from twenty

Years ago walking up the street with a miserable cheeseburger in one hand,
   & you
Imagine all this because you are still naive. The woman who brought her
The cheeseburger, the fries & coffee, the vanilla shake she sips after
   you've gone,

Is simply her lover. You are thinking of Berkeley & Telegraph
   Avenue in 1970
Because you cling to a belief in the Self, which memorizes, which
   is nothing,
Which grows over everything like the wild, cracked glaze of frost outside

As, once again, she puts her left nipple into the little hole in the glass.

2. Caravaggio: Swirl & Vortex

In the Borghese, Caravaggio, painter of boy whores, street punk,
  exile & murderer,
Left behind his own face in the decapitated, swollen, leaden-eyed head
  of Goliath,
And left the eyelids slightly open, & left on the face of David a look of
  pity

Mingling with disgust. A peach face; a death mask. If you look closely
  you can see
It is the same face, & the boy, murdering the man, is murdering his own
  boyhood,
His robe open & exposing a bare left shoulder. In 1603, it meant he was
  available,

For sale on the street where Ranuccio Tomassoni is falling, & Caravaggio,

Puzzled that a man would die so easily, turns & runs.

Wasn't it like this, after all? And this self-portrait, David holding him by
  a lock
Of hair? Couldn't it destroy time if he offered himself up like this,
  empurpled,
Bloated, the crime paid for in advance? To die before one dies, &
  keep painting?

This town, & that town, & exile? I stood there looking at it a long time.

A man whose only politics was rage. By 1970, tinted orchards &
  mass graves.

The song that closed the Fillmore was "Johnny B. Goode," as Garcia
  played it,
Without regret, the doors closing forever & the whole Haight evacuated,
  as if

Waiting for the touch of the renovator, for the new boutiques that
would open—

The patina of sunset glinting in the high, dark windows.

Once, I marched & linked arms with other exiles who wished to end
a war, & . . .
Sometimes, walking in that crowd, I became the crowd, &, for that
moment, it felt
Like entering the wide swirl & vortex of history. In the end,

Of course, you could either stay & get arrested, or else go home.

In the end, of course, the war finished without us in an empty row of
horse stalls

Littered with clothing that had been confiscated.

I had a friend in high school who looked like Caravaggio, or like Goliath—
Especially when he woke at dawn on someone's couch. (In early summer,
In California, half the senior class would skinny-dip & drink after midnight

In the unfinished suburb bordering the town, because, in the demonstration
models,
They filled the pools before the houses sold. . . . Above us, the lush stars
thickened.)
Two years later, thinking he heard someone call his name, he strolled
three yards

Off a path & stepped on a land mine.

Time's sovereign. It rides the backs of names cut into marble. And to get
Back, one must descend, as if into a mass grave. All along the memorial,
small

Offerings, letters, a bottle of bourbon, photographs, a joint of marijuana
   slipped

Into a wedding ring. You see, you must descend; it is one of the styles
Of Hell. And it takes a while to find the name you might be looking for;
   it is
Meant to take a while. You can touch the names, if you want to.
   You can kiss them,

You can try to tease out some final meaning with your lips.

The boy who was standing next to me said simply: "You can cry. . . .
   It's O.K., here."

"Whistlers," is what they called them. A doctor told me who'd worked
   the decks
Of a hospital ship anchored off Seoul. You could tell the ones who
   wouldn't last
By the sound, sometimes high-pitched as a coach's whistle, the wind
   made going

Through them. I didn't believe him at first, & so then he went into greater
Detail. . . . Some evenings, after there had been heavy casualties & a
   brisk wind,
He'd stare off a moment & think of a farm in Nebraska, of the way wheat

Bent in the wind below a slight rise, & no one around for miles.
   All he wanted,
He told me, after working in such close quarters for twelve hours,
   for sixteen
Hours, was that sudden sensation of spaciousness—wind, & no one there.

My friend, Zamora, used to chug warm vodka from the bottle, then execute
   a perfect
Reverse one-&-a-half gainer from the high board into the water.
   Sometimes,

When I think of him, I get confused. Someone is calling to him,
  & then

I'm actually thinking of Caravaggio . . . in his painting. I want to go
  up to it

And close both eyelids. They are still half open & it seems a little obscene

To leave them like that.

3. Turban

Sometimes, in the Brueghel paintings, the children who are skating
  hold perfectly
Still for a moment; I could have counted them there, if I wanted to.
  Or a boy
Has just fallen out of the sky, & no matter how hard the water is
  the splash

On the canvas is always silent, & can only grow more so. And the
  water rising
For centuries around the boy is famous only for the little silence it displays.
The way the paint has cracked slightly on the canvas is meant to remind you

That this is, after all, only a painting. In which Brueghel has destroyed time.
And Rembrandt, smiling at this, still has to put his house up for sale before
He can paint another self-portrait. This time he is St. Paul with a wry turban

On his head! There is a kind of forgiveness in it all. He looks as if he is
About to smile, but he does not, & then after a few moments it looks as if
He will never smile again. The turban is the dirty white of a popular beach.

4.   Our Sister of Perfect Solitude

In the Cathedral of Oaxaca, the usual women: three or four black
    shawls worn
To the iridescence of flies, the quaint agony of their prayers resembling
The buzzing of flies, &, on the sills, flies, & the emptiness of flies,

And the empty name rising upward in those prayers. Earlier,

At a café table, I saw a woman I once knew. She was wearing the same
    white silk
Skirt slit up the side, & was beginning to get drunk while her companion,
A boy of fourteen, the son of a weaver, was kissing her, & then, after a while,

Caressing her until soon a frank & unembarrassed tint of rose flushed
    her cheeks,
And a waiter glared at them both, then turned away, the white towel
    perfectly
Adjusted on his arm, before he spat, just once, into the street.

If you look at anything long enough, it turns into style.

One of my pastimes then was savoring the casual emptiness of names,
    any name,
Even the name of that stranger I said over & over in bed until her name
Slipped itself from all moorings, & her body became like wind stirring itself,

Until, free finally of its name, it would do anything.
And the next time I called her by another name, deliberately, just to see . . .
And repeated the name over & over until her body belonged to no one,
    to neither
One of us. It came to the same thing: without a name, the body could
    be anyone's,

Open to any suggestion.

This was the petty blasphemy I flirted with, the wind gusting over the
    empty tables.
I was learning how Guilt, feeding on the Body of Its Host, grows finally wise.
Which is another way of saying it grows terrified of anything as unscrupulous

As Itself, & then is simply mute, the shore of a lake clouding over.

Then it is best to go home.

But home is the form of the dream, & not the dream.

When you knock, the sill of tiny flowers trembles; no one's there; the woods
Around the cottage seem immense, as if they had grown in your absence,
    or were
A larger form of it, taking your place, their shade fallen forever, & colder. So,

To travel alone, to pick up & leave a town, to cling, for a moment, like dust; to
Collect as dust collects; is to move in the frank style of what passes.
But what remains, indwelling like a name not yours nor another's, persists

In the recurring dream of an animal, which loves you, which you cannot name.
Is it something that had a name before it could be given one?
Was the task of saying it a task assigned in childhood, its window sunlit
    & empty?

But the dream ends; the animal vanishes.

And the father, free finally of all fatherhood, stares out at an empty field
And wonders: is it dust, or ice? And is the spider its emissary, striding over
The freckled skin of an apple, & pausing there, harmless & brown & still,

A moment too long? And the apple itself? Is it dust or ice inside?

And the dream, with the work it cannot say?

And the sunlight's pressure on the empty window?

To go home is to take back a name. And to take a name back you must descend,
Even though you believe in no one; & even though the descent is into a woman, into
The empty hull of her myth, her body's vacancy after death, her perfect solitude—

Which is, & is not, this Church, the blood on the statue of Christ applied with
A bright red nail polish; & hands together, as, with luck, they will be in the end;
Or without luck they might be also, involuntarily, as in a prayer said backward,

To no one, to the crowd in the fitful shell game of all names, to the empty hush
Of the sun—cuffed & passing beneath it—painful when you move,

Painful when you do not move.

But what I did then was kneel & pray, &, after a while, lost track of the words
Or who it was for because somewhere in its sonorous repetitions I began hearing
The sound of trapped flies buzzing on the sill beneath stained glass . . .

And remembered a harness gall, some gnats hovering over it, on the withers

Of a horse, all its ribs showing as it hauled firewood on a towpath of lingering snowmelt.
In the summer its owner shot it through a graying left temple with a .22, for glue &
Tallow. And how it fell! Straight, fast, into a dry ditch

And onto the white, spreading sail of a canvas in which they wrapped &
   hoisted it,
Sail-like, the opaque, unreflecting yellow marble of its hooves hooked &
   tied—&
A last, faint odor, like a dignity, still clinging to its coat, a light wind riffling
   it just once.

And as the winch took hold & lifted it, the head loosened abruptly from its
   one dream; a glassy,
Piebald eye stared out at me, as if that stare could catch a world & put an end
To it, or set it afire. Dust & ice & a confetti of ashes. As if a horse could care!
   But then

The flies, swarming familiarly over its muzzle, nostrils & eyes, might as well
Have closed that eyelid, closed that eye as large as truth—which isn't all that
Large, or even truthful, & like that eye is often blue-gray, parti-colored
   or partly

Cloudy, & not necessarily human.

5. **"Coney Island Baby"**

But there is a place that will not change, a place that is rooted in dream;
It rots & rejoices; it flowers from nothing; it turns a deaf ear to millionaires:
You are seven, & the smell of raisins drying on a wicker tray is indescribable,
   & though the word *home*

Has a bomb ticking inside it, in its dream all objects slide back beneath their
   names again: shoe,
Hammer, rain, tea, delicate collarbones, paper, freckles, swan eyes, good-bye;
And later the last whirr & hush of a child's skate beneath the stars, & also

The moment after, cooling, which sounds like starlight. A street as simple as
A moon, & clothed in moonlight. Nude as moonlight. American styles.
   Dark leaf;
Light leaf; a girl in the loveliness of her name, the screen door banging once

Behind her as she runs out, & a stranger's impeccable wrists floating over a
keyboard:

What does it mean, American?

It means, mostly, to go unnoticed, to watch the streets filling with crowds,
& then
To step into the crowd, to *be* it suddenly, to type behind a desk all day
where no one
Sees you. To conceal all that you are. To perform your whole life in a silence

As deep as any girlhood is; to brim over like a black pond in summer, & say
nothing about it.
Sometimes it is too much & so you drift into unfamiliar streets, drift as hair
drifts along
A cheekbone, accentuating loss, a look of defeat in the eyes as you finger
a dress

On a rack, but you have no money. Your lips purse. It is 1931; it is 1931 again.

And suddenly this isn't about style anymore; this is something final like
beauty.

Friends, I'm going to stop right here because it is 1931 in her apartment
& no one's
Home. No one is coming home, either. After a while, I stop making inquiries.

After all, beauty has only three possible endings, & only one of them is
bearable.

The unthawed snow along the street is 1931; the screen door, banging, is 1931.

What does it mean but you? A wisp of hair below your ear, a little of 1931
In 1970, lost & unemployed. It means you just heard, from the open window
Of an apartment overhead, twelve bars, "Autumn Leaves," as played by
someone noble,

Untiring, explosive, & extinct. And suddenly the raw light above the arms
    of snow
'Outstretched upon the street is bearable, you think, & will be bearable. For
Another two hours it might be bearable to walk beside it, as if beside a
    companion

Who's always there, who's always disappearing into light, which is to say,
Into Himself. Who leaves you the afternoon & the tavern's darkness where
    you hope
To find work. The funny sayings along the wall are not so funny, once you

Think about them, & up at one end, a tiny stage, & always the two or three
Regular drinkers with their silence as if their silence were a rare & precious
    thing,
Inviolate & white despite its bruises, as if, at night a thing inside themselves

Had beaten them past all recognition, as if, above the cold pews of a church,
Above that body which sails yet holds quite still, each one had seen,
    set deep
Into the hacked, carved, crucified wooden face, too large & too obscene
    to match

The half-closed other, a piebald horse's eye. And each had turned away.

And this? This is the most unscrupulous thing of all. These scratchings
    all night,
These inquiries because you are not there, have become, simply, you,
    white paper
Desiring the darkening effects of ink until, late at night, it is black trees,

White snow. A winter landscape, & the hush when I come back to it as bitter
    & serene
As coffee, solitude, the first snow grazing the streets. It is pure, the way
    cruelty is pure.

I swear I'd give the whole thing up for you.

6. As It Begins with a Brush Stroke on a Snare Drum

The plaza was so still in that moment two years ago that everything
   was clear,
As if it had been preserved beneath a kind of lacquered stillness, &,
   for a while,
I did not even notice the pigeons lifting above the sad tiles of churches,

Or how they must have sounded like applause that is not meant for anyone;

I must not have noticed that blind woman on the corner who begged
   coins for
A living, who had one eye swelled shut entirely while the other was held
Wide open to witness spittle on the curb . . . a thin film of glaucoma
   over it

That had taken on the lustreless sheen of a nickel. And soon the band
In their sun-bleached military uniforms was tuning up beneath the
   blossom of rust
Covering the gazebo, its eaves festooned with the off-white spiderwebs
   of unlit Christmas lights.

And that girl, Socorro, her smile surfacing voluptuously as an unspoken
   thought

Again, was selling gardenias—their petals already beginning to appear
Faintly discolored around the edges—from a basket she carried on her head
In an unwobbling stillness; Martín was selling Chiclets but no one bought

Chiclets anymore; no one bought the little squawking birds or the
   cheap stone
Animals turned out on a lathe in Veracruz, either; no one wanted his
   shoes shined.
By then the band was playing show tunes from *My Fair Lady* & *South
   Pacific* & was

Interrupted only once because of a routine demonstration by the
   Communists, who,

Mostly, were demonstrating because it was Sunday & because that is what
  they did,
On Sundays. After a while I started walking vaguely away beside some
  fading stonework,

Which in fact is not called Our Lady of Perfect Solitude nor even Our Sister
Of Perpetual Solitude, but simply Santo Domingo. I do not know why I
  walked near it then,
And passed it without entering.

Still, in the painting, the children kept skating, & the others are probably
Walking home from school at this moment in their yellow raincoats, with
The stale smells left on wax paper locked in their lunch pails. That woman

Keeps brushing her hair, & so somewhere it is still 1970 & the riot police
Are spilling out of their buses. On the marsh above the sound there were
  egrets,
There were black swans nesting in the rushes; the canal was warm & salty.

There was a cabin filling with so much moonlight I almost believed I could
Dissolve in it if I sat very still, & I sat very still. I watched my son
Skating at the edge of a pond in his sleep. It was summer by the time

I finally saw the painting in Vienna & counted each one of the children as if
To make sure they were still there, then gradually lost count, & in the dream
Of the plowman on the hill there must have been the face of an English poet

Looking as lined as a maple leaf pressed between the pages of a book.
  Beneath it
The Danube is gliding, & I am just holding his book now, not even needing
  to read it
Anymore as I cross into the frontier—green wheat, alfalfa, a feeling
  of distance

In it all like sleep or rain reclaiming some lost, rural Missouri slum
  town until

It no longer exists—& now the Hungarian checkpoint, where guards
  with stars
The shade of American lipstick on their caps will enter & seem proud of
  the unchipped,

Deep blue enamel on their machine guns. Most of them are just poor
  teenagers
From the surrounding villages & farms . . . & innocent, &

                    The only glamour that is left
                    On the Orient Express
                    Is a soiled, torn doily on an armrest.

Rhyme then, rhyme & dream, but in the other painting, which is not
  a painting,
They are trudging home from school in the rain which is like a kind
  of sleep
When one of them thinks the mind is not the mind in the unbewitched,
  meticulous,

First shaping of numbers on a blackboard; it is only the shadow of a
  skater over
A white pond. There is a sea beyond it, roughened by whitecaps, &
  the mind
Moves first one way, then another, then both ways at once, & then
  one long

Glide past the pines that look black from this far away, but aren't black.
The boy's friend is saying he "hates school, but only sort of." But the boy's
Not listening, he is thinking that something he painted was something
  he dreamt,

And then some of the dream got mixed in with the paint, & then
  with recess,
The afternoon, this long walk in the rain, & now he will never get it sorted
Out. . . . In the story, the boy, falling, must have thought his father had wings

Unlike his own, & real. That is why the myth is so clear, & so cruel, &
Why we survive it. Yellow rain gear. Black woods. Gray sky. Home
Is where you can forget some things, the boy is thinking, because he is

Tired from having to walk for so long & because he has left his galoshes
At school & his shoes are wet as he unthinkingly turns his back to me now,
Goes up the worn, slick steps of a front porch, & the door closes. And,

Because I am not allowed to see it, there is a glass of milk on the table,
The stairs behind it are dark, & from a narrow upstairs window there is
A glimpse of the sea, & later, in his dream, there is sometimes a father.

And then it is more like a story about a father, & then it is the hush of ice
Over a pond's surface. In spring, when it begins to thaw, there is a little
Noise underneath it like steel sighing, if steel could sigh as it seems to,

Sometimes, when you are walking home alone on a trestle above a river &
    there
Is a broken pattern of geese above it, a "V" decomposing, a sky mottled
    with blue
And some clouds. It is like a father dissolving, & setting you free, & what

Has the father ever achieved that will outlast his own vanishing? And so
The boy spits over the railing & watches the silvery web of it falling
And thinning until it is gossamer, a filament untying itself forever & saying

Exactly what forever always meant to say—that this long pull of spring tide
    in the river
Needs nothing, nothing except its one momentary witness, a boy pausing

Above it all on a bridge.

In Oaxaca, after the bomb went off, there were nevertheless a few
    seconds . . . a
Pure stillness in which I could hear the fountain in the plaza, distant traffic,
The sudden silence of birds. Then everyone was rushing through the streets

Toward a place where sound had been, a place that wasn't there. It is funny,
But the sound of a bomb, a few seconds after it has gone off, is no longer
   even
Surprising. In a little while it seems only right, & sad. I sat in the balcony of
   a restaurant

Overlooking it all, & read a poem by Alberto Blanco in the magazine edited
   by Paz,
And waited for the place to open, & in the next hour I watched the plaza
Gradually fill with the usual crowds . . . those who love, or those who think
   they love,

Novelty, & change.

7. Coda: Kind of Blue

And *So what?* said a trumpet; & *I'll see you that & raise you five,* said a kind
Of rippling laughter, gone now, on the keyboard; & *Well just this once,* the
   bass
Replied; *Maybe again, maybe not,* a brush stroke swore on a snare & high
   hat. Styles

As American as loss: *I'm going to say what the snow says, falling on the tracks*
Outside Chicago, & then I'll unsay that. I'll dissolve this city, wall by blackened
Wall, & Mr. Grief & Ms. Beauty, I'll build a new one from your names. Ashes,

My name is Mr. John Coltrane,
Sweet insolence, & rain.
I don't come back again.

And *Am I Blue? So what? You think I didn't know what time it was?* said the
   trumpet.
Take her hair, some smoke & snow, & give it all one name. Style it as you
   please
Take someone who can't stop screaming, the el overhead, the sky, & give it
   a name.

Take Charlie Parker's grave all overgrown with weeds in Kansas City. Add
    nothing,
Except an ocher tint of shame. May all your Christmases be white & Bird be
    still
In L.A., gone, broken, insane. Take Beauty before her habit mutes & cripples
    her,

Then add some grief. But don't change a thing this time, not even a white
    gardenia
Pressed against her ear. Not even one syllable of her name. "In my solitude"
Is how the song began. All things you are, & briefly, as, in solitude, it ends.

Prince Jesus, crush those bastards . . .

—François Villon, *Grand Testament*

It is the unremarkable that will last,

As in Brueghel's camouflage, where the wren's withheld,
While elsewhere on a hill, small hawks (or are they other birds?)
Are busily unraveling eyelashes & pupils
From sunburned thieves outstretched on scaffolds,
Their last vision obscured by wings, then broken, entered.
I cannot tell whether their blood spurts, or just spills,
Their faces are wings, & their bodies are uncovered.

The twittering they hear is the final trespass.

And all later luxuries—the half-dressed neighbor couple
Shouting insults at each other just beyond
Her bra on a cluttered windowsill, then ceasing it when
A door was slammed to emphasize, like trouble,

The quiet flowing into things then, spreading its wake
From the child's toy left out on a lawn
To the broken treatise of jet-trails drifting above—seem
Keel scrapes on the shores of some enlarging mistake,

A wrong so wide no one can speak of it now in the town
That once had seemed, like its supporting factories
That manufactured poems & weaponry,
Like such a good idea. And wasn't it everyone's?

Wasn't the sad pleasure of assembly lines a replica
Of the wren's perfect, camouflaged self-sufficiency,

And of its refusal even to be pretty,
Surviving in a plumage dull enough to blend in with

A hemline of smoke, sky, & a serene indifference?

The dead wren I found on a gravel drive
One morning, all beige above and off-white
Underneath, the body lighter, no more than a vacant tent

Of oily feathers stretched, blent, & lacquered shut
Against the world—was a world I couldn't touch.
And in its skull a snow of lice had set up such
An altar, the congregation spreading from the tongue

To round, bare sills that had been its eyes, I let
It drop, my hand changed for a moment
By a thing so common it was never once distracted from
The nothing all wrens meant, the one feather on the road.

No feeding in the wake of cavalry or kings changed it.
Even in the end it swerved away, & made the abrupt
Riddle all things come to seem . . . irrelevant:
The tucked claws clutched emptiness like a stick.

And if Death whispered as always in the language of curling
Leaves, or a later one that makes us stranger,
"Don't you come *near* me motherfucker";
If the tang of metal in slang made the New World fertile,

Still . . . as they resumed their quarrel in the quiet air,
I could hear the species cheep in what they said . . .
Until their voices rose. Until the sound of a slap erased
A world, & the woman, in a music stripped of all prayer,

Began sobbing, & the man become bystander cried *O Jesus.*

In the sky, the first stars were already faint
And timeless, but what could they matter to that boy, blent
To no choir, who saw at last the clean wings of indifferent

Hunger, & despair? Around him the other petty thieves,

With arms outstretched, & eyes pecked out by birds, reclined,
Fastened forever to scaffolds which gradually would cover
An Empire's hills & line its roads as far
As anyone escaping in a cart could see, his swerving mind

On the dark brimming up in everything, the reins
Going slack in his hand as the cart slows, & stops,
And the horse sees its own breath go out
Onto the cold air, & gazes after the off-white plume,

And seems amazed by it, by its breath, by everything.
But the man slumped behind it, dangling a lost nail
Between his lips, only stares at the swishing tail,
At each white breath going out, thinning, & then vanishing,

For he has grown tired of amazing things.

The Carpathian Frontier, October, 1968

—for my brother

Once, in a foreign country, I was suddenly ill.
I was driving south toward a large city famous
For so little it had a replica, in concrete,
In two-thirds scale, of the Arc de Triomphe stuck
In the midst of traffic, & obstructing it.
But the city was hours away, beyond the hills
Shaped like the bodies of sleeping women.
Often I had to slow down for herds of goats
Or cattle milling on those narrow roads, & for
The narrower, lost, stone streets of villages
I passed through. The pains in my stomach had grown
Gradually sharper & more frequent as the day
Wore on, & now a fever had set up house.
In the villages there wasn't much point in asking
Anyone for help. In those places, where tanks
Were bivouacked in shade on their way back
From some routine exercise along
The Danube, even food was scarce that year.
And the languages shifted for no clear reason
From two hard quarries of Slavic into German,
Then to a shred of Latin spliced with oohs
And hisses. Even when I tried the simplest phrases,
The peasants passing over those uneven stones
Paused just long enough to look up once,
Uncomprehendingly. Then they turned
Quickly away, vanishing quietly into that
Moment, like bark chips whirled downriver.
It was autumn. Beyond each village the wind
Threw gusts of yellowing leaves across the road.
The goats I passed were thin, gray; their hind legs,
Caked with dried shit, seesawed along—

Not even the mild contempt in their expressionless,
Pale eyes, & their brays like the scraping of metal.
Except for one village that had a kind
Of museum where I stopped to rest, & saw
A dead Scythian soldier under glass,
Turning to dust while holding a small sword
At attention forever, there wasn't much to look at.
Wind, leaves, goats, the higher passes
Locked into stone, the peasants with their fate
Embroidering a stillness into them,
And a spell over all things in that landscape,
Like. . . .
                    That was the trouble; it couldn't be
Compared to anything else, not even the sleep
Of some asylum at a wood's edge with the sound
Of a pond's spillway beside it. But as each cramp
Grew worse & lasted longer than the one before,
It was hard to keep myself aloof from the threadbare
World walking on that road. After all,
Even as they moved, the peasants, the herds of goats
And cattle, the spiraling leaves, at least were part
Of that spell, that stillness.
                                        After a while,
The villages grew even poorer, then thinned out,
Then vanished entirely. An hour later,
There were no longer even the goats, only wind,
Then more & more leaves blown over the road, sometimes
Covering it completely for a second.
And yet, except for a random oak or some brush
Writhing out of the ravine I drove beside,
The trees had thinned into rock, into large,
Tough blonde rosettes of fading pasture grass.
Then *that* gave out in a bare plateau. . . . And then,
Easing the Dacia down a winding grade
In second gear, rounding a long, funneled curve—
In a complete stillness of yellow leaves filling
A wide field—like something thoughtlessly,
Mistakenly erased, the road simply ended.

I stopped the car. There was no wind now.
I expected that, & though I was sick & lost,
I wasn't afraid. I should have been afraid.
To this day I don't know why I wasn't.
I could hear time cease, the field quietly widen.
I could feel the spreading stillness of the place
Moving like something I'd witnessed as a child,
Like the ancient, armored leisure of some reptile
Gliding, gray-yellow, into the slightly tepid,
Unidentical gray-brown stillness of the water—
Something blank & unresponsive in its tough,
Pimpled skin—seen only a moment, then unseen
As it submerged to rest on mud, or glided just
Beneath the lustreless, calm yellow leaves
That clustered along a log, or floated there
In broken ringlets, held by a gray froth
On the opaque, unbroken surface of the pond,
Which reflected nothing, no one.
                              And then I remembered.
When I was a child, our neighbors would disappear.
And there wasn't a pond of crocodiles at all.
And they hadn't moved. They couldn't move. They
Lived in the small, fenced-off backwater
Of a canal. I'd never seen them alive. They
Were in still photographs taken on the Ivory Coast.
I saw them only once in a studio when
I was a child in a city I once loved.
I was afraid until our neighbor, a photographer,
Explained it all to me, explained how far
Away they were, how harmless; how they were praised
In rituals as "powers." But they had no "powers,"
He said. The next week he vanished. I thought
Someone had cast a spell & that the crocodiles
Swam out of the pictures on the wall & grew
Silently & multiplied & then turned into
Shadows resting on the banks of lakes & streams
Or took the shapes of fallen logs in campgrounds
In the mountains. They ate our neighbor, Mr. Hirata.

They ate his whole family. That is what I believed,
Then . . . that someone had cast a spell. I did not
Know childhood was a spell, or that then there
Had been another spell, too quiet to hear,
Entering my city, entering the dust we ate. . . .
No one knew it then. No one could see it,
Though it spread through lawnless miles of housing tracts,
And the new, bare, treeless streets; it slipped
Into the vacant rows of warehouses & picked
The padlocked doors of working-class bars
And union halls & shuttered, empty diners.
And how it clung! (forever, if one had noticed)
To the brothel with the pastel tassels on the shade
Of an unlit table lamp. Farther in, it feasted
On the decaying light of failing shopping centers;
It spilled into the older, tree-lined neighborhoods,
Into warm houses, sealing itself into books
Of bedtime stories read each night by fathers—
The books lying open to the flat, neglected
Light of dawn; & it settled like dust on windowsills
Downtown, filling the smug cafés, schools,
Banks, offices, taverns, gymnasiums, hotels,
Newsstands, courtrooms, opium parlors, Basque
Restaurants, Armenian steam baths,
French bakeries, & two of the florists' shops—
Their plate glass windows smashed forever.
Finally it tried to infiltrate the exact
Center of my city, a small square bordered
With palm trees, olives, cypresses, a square
Where no one gathered, not even thieves or lovers.
It was a place which no longer had any purpose,
But held itself aloof, I thought, the way
A deaf aunt might, from opinions, styles, gossip.
I liked it there. It was completely lifeless,
Sad & clear in what seemed always a perfect,
Windless noon. I saw it first as a child,
Looking down at it from that as yet
Unvandalized, makeshift studio.

I remember leaning my right cheek against
A striped beach ball so that Mr. Hirata—
Who was Japanese, who would be sent the next week
To a place called Manzanar, a detention camp
Hidden in stunted pines almost above
The Sierra timberline—could take my picture.
I remember the way he lovingly relished
Each camera angle, the unwobbling tripod,
The way he checked each aperture against
The light meter, in love with all things
That were not accidental, & I remember
The care he took when focusing; how
He tried two different lens filters before
He found the one appropriate for that
Sensual, late, slow blush of afternoon
Falling through the one broad bay window.
I remember holding still & looking down
Into the square because he asked me to;
Because my mother & father had asked me please
To obey & be patient & allow the man—
Whose business was failing anyway by then—
To work as long as he wished to without any
Irritations or annoyances before
He would have to spend these years, my father said,
Far away, in snow, & without his cameras.
But Mr. Hirata did not work. He played.
His toys gleamed there. That much was clear to me. . . .
That was the day I decided I would never work.
It felt like a conversion. Play was sacred.
My father waited behind us on a sofa made
From car seats. One spring kept nosing through.
I remember the camera opening into the light. . . .
And I remember the dark after, the studio closed,
The cameras stolen, slivers of glass from the smashed
Bay window littering the unsanded floors,
And the square below it bathed in sunlight. . . . All this
Before Mr. Hirata died, months later,
From complications following pneumonia.

His death, a letter from a camp official said,
Was purely accidental. I didn't believe it.
Diseases were wise. Diseases, like the polio
My sister had endured, floating paralyzed
And strapped into her wheelchair all through
That war, seemed too precise. Like photographs . . .
Except disease left nothing. Disease was like
An equation that drank up light & never ended,
Not even in summer. Before my fever broke,
And the pains lessened, I could actually see
Myself, in the exact center of that square.
How still it had become in my absence, & how
Immaculate, windless, sunlit. I could see
The outline of every leaf on the nearest tree,
See it more clearly than ever, more clearly than
I had seen anything before in my whole life:
Against the modest, dark gray, solemn trunk,
The leaves were becoming only what they had to be—
Calm, yellow, things in themselves & nothing
More—& frankly they were nothing in themselves,
Nothing except their little reassurance
Of persisting for a few more days, or returning
The year after, & the year after that, & every
Year following—estranged from us by now—& clear,
So clear not one in a thousand trembled; hushed
And always coming back—steadfast, orderly,
Taciturn, oblivious—until the end of Time.

At the Grave of My Guardian Angel:
St. Louis Cemetery, New Orleans

for Gerald Stern

At sixteen I was so vulnerable to every influence
That the overcast light, making the trash of addicts & sunbathers
    suddenly clearer
On the paths of the city park, seemed death itself spreading its shade
Over the leaves, the swan boats, the gum wrappers, and the quarreling
    ducks.
It took nothing more than a few clouds straying over the sun,
And I would begin falling through myself like an anvil or a girl's comb or
    a feather
Dropped, tossed, or spiraling by pure chance down the silent air shaft of
    a warehouse,
The spiderweb in one fourth-floor window catching, in that moment,
    the sunset.
For in such a moment, to fall was to be simplified & pure,
With a neck snapped like a stem instead
Of whoever I turned out to be,
Wiping the window glass clear with one cuff
To gaze out at a two-hundred-year-old live oak tethering
The courtyard to its quiet,
The tree so old it has outlived even its life as a cliché,
And has survived, with no apparent effort, every boy who marched, like a
    wilderness
Himself, past it on his way to enlist in Lee's army,
And now it swells gently in the mist & the early sunlight.
So who saved me? And for what purpose?
Beneath the small angel cut from cheap stone, there was nothing
But my name & the years 1947–1949,
And the tense, muggy little quiet of a place where singing ends,
And where there is only the leftover colored chalk & the delusions of
    voodoo,
The small bones & X's on stones signifying the practitioner's absence,
Entirely voluntary, from the gnat swirl & humming of time;

To which the chalked X on stone is the final theory; it is even illiterate.
It is not even a lock of hair on a grave. It is not even
The small crowd of roughnecks at Poe's funeral, nor the blind drunkard
Laughing there, the white of his eyes the unfurling of a cold surf below a
    cliff—
Which is the blank wave sprawl of fact receding under the cries of gulls—
Which is not enough.

I should rush out to my office & eat a small, freckled apple leftover
From 1970 & entirely wizened & rotted by sunlight now,
Then lay my head on my desk & dream again of horses grazing, riderless
    & still saddled,
Under the smog of the freeway cloverleaf & within earshot of the music
    waltzing with itself out
Of the topless bars & laundromats of East L.A.

I should go back again & try to talk my friend out of his diet
Of methamphetamine & vodka yogurts & the look of resignation
    spreading over his face
Like the gray shade of a tree spreading over a sleeper in the park—

For it is all or nothing in this life, for there is no other.
And without beauty, Bakunin will go on making his forlorn &
    unreliable little bombs in the cold, & Oswald will adjust
The lenses on the scope of his rifle, the one
Friend he has carried with him all the way out of his childhood,
The silent wood of its stock as musical to him in its grain as any violin.
This must have been what they meant,
Lincoln & Whitman, joining hands one overcast spring afternoon
To stroll together through the mud of Washington at the end
Of the war, the tears welling up in both their eyes,
Neither one of them saying a word, their hands clasped tightly together
As they walk for block after block past
The bay, sorrel, chestnut, and dapple-gray tail swish of horses,
And waiting carriages, & neither one of them noticing, as they stroll
    & weave,

The harness gall on the winters of a mare,
Nor the gnats swarming over it, alighting now on the first trickle of blood
    uncaking from the sore;
And the underfed rib cage showing through its coat each time it inhales
Like the tines of a rake combing the battleground to overturn
Something that might identify the dead at Antietam.
The rake keeps flashing in the late autumn light.
And Bakunin, with a face impassive as a barn owl's & never straying from
    the one true text of flames?
And Lincoln, absentmindedly trying to brush away the wart on his cheek
As he dresses for the last time,
As he fumbles for a pair of cuff links in a silk-lined box,
As he anticipates some pure & frivolous pleasure,
As he dreams for a moment, & is a woman for a moment,
And in his floating joy has no idea what is going to happen to him in the
    next hour?
And Oswald dozing over a pamphlet by Trotsky in the student union?
Oh live oak, thoughtless beauty in a century of pulpy memoirs,
Spreading into the early morning sunlight
As if it could never be otherwise, as if it were all a pure proclamation of
    leaves & a final quiet—

But it's all or nothing in this life; it's smallpox, quicklime, & fire.
It's the extinct whistling of an infantry; it is all the faded rosettes of blood
Turning into this amnesia of billboards & the ceaseless *hunh?* of traffic.
It goes on & I go with it; it spreads into the sun & air & throws out a fast
    shade
That will never sleep, and I go with it; it breaks Lincoln & Poe into small
    drops of oil spreading
Into endless swirls on the water, & I recognize the pattern:

There there now, Nothing.
Stop your sniveling. Stop sifting dirt through your fingers into your glass
    of milk,

A milk still white as stone; whiter even. Why don't you finish it?
We'd better be getting on our way soon, sweet Nothing.
I'll buy you something pretty from the store.
I'll let you wear the flower in your hair even though you can only vanish
    entirely underneath its brown, implacable petals.
Stop your sniveling. I can almost see the all night diner looming
Up ahead, with its lights & its flashing sign a testimony to failure.
I can almost see our little apartment under the freeway overpass, the cups on
    the mantle rattling continually—
The Mojave one way; the Pacific the other.
At least we'll have each other's company.
And it's not as if you held your one wing, tattered as it was, in contempt
For being only one. It's not as if you were frivolous.
It's not like that. It's not like that at all.
Riding beside me, your seat belt around your invisible waist. Sweet Nothing.
Sweet, sweet Nothing.

Elegy

My name in Latin is light to carry & victorious.
I'd read late in the library, then
Walk out past the stacks, rows, aisles

Of books, where the memoirs of battles slowly gave way
To case histories of molestation & abuse.

The black widows looked out onto the black lawn.

Friends, in the middle of this life, I was embraced
By failure. It clung to me & did not let go.
When I ran, brother limitation raced

Beside me like a shadow. Have you never
Felt like this, everyone you know,

Turning, the more they talked, into . . .

Acquaintances? So many strong opinions!

And when I tried to speak—
Someone always interrupting. My head ached.
And I would walk home in the blackness of winter.

I still had two friends, but they were trees.
One was a box elder, the other a horse chestnut.

I used to stop on my way home & talk to each

Of them. The three of us lived in Utah then, though
We never learned why, me, *acer negundo,* & the other
One, whose name I can never remember.

"Everything I have done has come to nothing.
It is not even worth mocking," I would tell them,
And then I would look up into their limbs & see

How they were covered in ice. "You do not even
Have a car anymore," one of them would answer.

All their limbs glistening above me,
No light was as cold or clear.

I got over it, but I was never the same,

Hearing the snow change to rain & the wind swirl,
And the gull's cry, that it could not fly out of.

In time, in a few months, I could walk beneath
Both trees without bothering to look up
Anymore, neither at the one

Whose leaves & trunk were being slowly colonized by
Birds again, nor at the other, sleepier, more slender

One, that seemed frail, but was really

Oblivious to everything. Simply oblivious to it,
With the pale leaves climbing one side of it,
An obscure sheen in them,

And the other side, for some reason, black, bare,
The same, almost irresistible, carved indifference

In the shape of its limbs

As if someone's cries for help
Had been muffled by them once, concealed there,

Her white flesh just underneath the slowly peeling bark

—while the joggers swerved around me & I stared—

Still tempting me to step in, find her,

                    And possess her completely.

Some called it the Summer of Love; & although the clustered,
Motionless leaves that overhung the streets looked the same
As ever, the same as they did every summer, in 1967,
Anybody with three dollars could have a vision.
And who wouldn't want to know what it felt like to be
A cedar waxwing landing with a flutter of gray wings
In a spruce tree, & then disappearing into it,
For only three dollars? And now I know; its flight is ecstasy.
No matter how I look at it, I also now know that
The short life of a cedar waxwing is more pure pleasure
Than anyone alive can still be sane, & bear.
And remember, a cedar waxwing doesn't mean a thing,
Qua cedar or *qua* waxwing, nor could it have earned
That kind of pleasure by working to become a better
Cedar waxwing. They're all the same.
Show me a bad cedar waxwing, for example, & I mean
A really morally corrupted cedar waxwing, & you'll commend
The cage they have reserved for you, resembling heaven.

Some people spent their lives then, having visions.
But in my case, the morning after I dropped mescaline
I had to spray Johnson grass in a vineyard of Thompson Seedless
My father owned—& so, still feeling the holiness of all things
Living, holding the spray gun in one hand & driving with the other,
The tractor pulling the spray rig & its sputtering motor—
Row after row, I sprayed each weed I found
That looked enough like Johnson grass, a thing alive that's good
For nothing at all, with a mixture of malathion & diesel fuel,
And said to each tall weed, as I coated it with a lethal mist,
Dominus vobiscum, &, sometimes, *mea culpa,* until
It seemed boring to apologize to weeds, & insincere as well.
For in a day or so, no more than that, the weeds would turn
Disgusting hues of yellowish orange & wither away. I still felt
The bird's flight in my body when I thought about it, the wing ache,

Lifting heaven, locating itself somewhere just above my slumped
Shoulders, & part of me taking wing. I'd feel it at odd moments
After that on those long days I spent shoveling vines, driving trucks
And tractors, helping swamp fruit out of one orchard
Or another, but as the summer went on, I felt it less & less.

As the summer went on, some were drafted, some enlisted
In a generation that would not stop falling, a generation
Of leaves sticking to body bags, & when they turned them
Over, they floated back to us on television, even then,
In the Summer of Love, in 1967,
When riot police waited beyond the doors of perception,
And the best thing one could do was get arrested.

At Wilshire & Santa Monica I saw an opossum
Trying to cross the street. It was late, the street
Was brightly lit, the opossum would take
A few steps forward, then back away from the breath
Of moving traffic. People coming out of the bars
Would approach, as if to help it somehow.
It would lift its black lips & show them
The reddened gums, the long rows of incisors,
Teeth that went all the way back beyond
The flames of Troy & Carthage, beyond sheep
Grazing rock-strewn hills, fragments of ruins
In the grass at San Vitale. It would back away
Delicately & smoothly, stepping carefully
As it always had. It could mangle someone's hand
In twenty seconds. Mangle it for good. It could
Sever it completely from the wrist in forty.
There was nothing to be done for it. Someone
Or other probably called the LAPD, who then
Called Animal Control, who woke a driver, who
Then dressed in mailed gloves, the kind of thing
Small knights once wore into battle, who gathered
Together his pole with a noose on the end,
A light steel net to snare it with, someone who hoped
The thing would have vanished by the time he got there.

The brow of a horse in that moment when
The horse is drinking water so deeply from a trough
It seems to inhale the water, is holy.

I refuse to explain.

When the horse had gone the water in the trough,
All through the empty summer,

Went on reflecting clouds & stars.

The horse cropping grass in a field,
And the fly buzzing around its eyes, are more real
Than the mist in one corner of the field.

Or the angel hidden in the mist, for that matter.

Members of the Committee on the Ineffable,
Let me illustrate this with a story, & ask you all
To rest your heads on the table, cushioned,
If you wish, in your hands, &, if you want,
Comforted by a small carton of milk
To drink from, as you once did, long ago,
When there was only a curriculum of beach grass,
When the University of Flies was only a distant humming.

In Romania, after the war, Stalin confiscated
The horses that had been used to work the fields.
"You won't need horses now," Stalin said, cupping
His hand to his ear, "Can't you hear the tractors
Coming in the distance? I hear them already."

The crowd in the Callea Victoria listened closely
But no one heard anything. In the distance

There was only the faint glow of a few clouds.
And the horses were led into boxcars & emerged
As the dimly remembered meals of flesh
That fed the starving Poles
During that famine, & part of the next one—
In which even words grew thin & transparent,

Like the pale wings of ants that flew
Out of the oldest houses, & slowly
What had been real in words began to be replaced
By what was not real, by the not exactly real.
"Well, not exactly, but . . ." became the preferred
Administrative phrasing so that the man
Standing with his hat in his hands would not guess
That the phrasing of a few words had already swept
The earth from beneath his feet. "That horse I had,
He was more real than any angel,
The housefly, when I had a house, was real too,"
Is what the man thought.
Yet it wasn't more than a few months
Before the man began to wonder, talking
To himself out loud before the others,
"Was the horse real? Was the house real?"
An angel flew in and out of the high window
In the factory where the man worked, his hands
Numb with cold. He hated the window & the light
Entering the window & he hated the angel.
Because the angel could not be carved into meat
Or dumped into the ossuary & become part
Of the landfill at the edge of town,
It therefore could not acquire a soul,
And resembled in significance nothing more
Than a light summer dress when the body has gone.

The man survived because, after a while,
He shut up about it.

Stalin had a deep understanding of the *kulaks,*
Their sense of marginalization & belief in the land;

That is why he killed them all.

Members of the Committee on Solitude, consider
Our own impoverishment & the progress of that famine,
In which, now, it is becoming impossible
To feel anything when we contemplate the burial,
Alive, in a two-hour period, of hundreds of people.

Who were not clichés, who did not know they would be
The illegible blank of the past that lives in each
Of us, even in some guy watering his lawn

On a summer night. Consider

The death of Stalin & the slow, uninterrupted
Evolution of the horse, a species no one,
Not even Stalin, could extinguish, almost as if
What could not be altered was something
Noble in the look of its face, something

Incapable of treachery.

Then imagine, in your planning proposals,
The exact moment in the future when an angel
Might alight & crawl like a fly into the ear of a horse,
And then, eventually, into the brain of a horse,
And imagine further that the angel in the brain
Of this horse is, for the horse cropping grass
In the field, largely irrelevant, a mist in the corner
Of the field, something that disappears,
The horse thinks, when weight is passed through it,
Something that will not even carry the weight
Of its own father

On its back, the horse decides, & so demonstrates
This by swishing at a fly with its tail, by continuing
To graze as the dusk comes on & almost until it is night.

Old contrivers, daydreamers, walking chemistry sets,
Exhausted chimneysweeps of the spaces
Between words, where the Holy Ghost tastes just
Like the dust it is made of,
Let's tear up our lecture notes & throw them out
The window.
Let's do it right now before wisdom descends upon us
Like a spiderweb over a burned-out theater marquee,
Because what's the use?
I keep going to meetings where no one's there,
And contributing to the discussion.

And besides, behind the angel hissing in its mist
Is a gate that leads only into another field,
Another outcropping of stones & withered grass, where
A horse named Sandman & a horse named Anastasia
Used to stand at the fence & watch the traffic pass.
Where there were outdoor concerts once, in summer,
Under the missing & innumerable stars.

When my friends found me after I'd been blown
Into the limbs of a tree, my arms were wide open.
It must have looked as if I were welcoming something,

Awakening to it. They left my arms like that,
Not because of the triumphant, mocking shape they took
In death, & not because the withheld breath

Of death surprised my arms, made them believe,
For a split second, that they were really wings
Instead of arms, & had always been wings. No, it was

Because, by the time the others found me, I had been
Sitting there for hours with my arms spread wide,
And when they tried, they couldn't bend them back,

Couldn't cross them over my chest as was the custom,
So that the corpses that kept lining the tracks
Might look like sleeping choir boys. They were

No choir, although in death they were restored
To all they had been once. They were just boys
Fading back into the woods & the ravines again.

I could see that much in the stingy, alternating light
And shade the train threw out as it began to slow,
And the rest of us gazed out from what seemed to me

One endless, empty window on what had to be.
What had to be came nearer in a sudden hiss of brakes,
The glass clouding with our reflections as we stood.

Arms & wings. They'll mock you one way or the other.

Boy in Video Arcade

Some see a lake of fire at the end of it,
Or heaven's guesswork, something always to be sketched in.

I see a sullen boy in a video arcade.
He's the only one there at this hour, shoulders slightly bent above a machine.
I see the pimples on his chin, the scuffed linoleum on the floor.

I like the close-up, the detail. I like the pointlessness of it,
And the way it hasn't imagined an ending to all this yet,

The boy never bothering to look up as the sun comes out
In the late morning, because, Big Deal, the mist evaporating & rising.

So Death blows his little fucking trumpet, Big Deal, says the boy.

I don't see anything at the end of it except an endlessness,

The beauty parlors, the palm reader's unlighted sign, the mulberry trees
Fading out before the billboard of the chiropractor.

The lake of fire's just an oil speck.
I don't see anything at the end of it, & I suppose that is what is wrong
     with me,

Among the other things. And it's slow work, because of all the gauzy light,

It's hard to pick out anything.

Because they could not blind him twice, they drove a pencil
Through the blind king's ear. The pencil could not believe the thing
It had been asked to do, but by then it was already entering the mind,

And there it forgot that it had ever been a pencil.

Darkness reigned in the basement of the record store in Ogden, Utah,
Where all this happened, & there wasn't any king. The other king, the one who
Came in the night, was blind & mad, & owned a record store. And was a
    Mormon.

So were his ungrateful daughters who would pretend to pry his eyes out
With kitchen spoons, & so, within the kingdom, was everyone except
The Fool who repaired chainsaws & snowmobiles & thought of them as small,

Snarling gods whose faith & hatred of trees was perfect. The man who owned

the record store had once suspected God did not exist & had spent a summer
Lying on the beach at Santa Monica trying hard not to believe in God,
And was unable to. It was 1967. *Wild Thing* was coming from a radio. Her
    name

Was Dawn. She had dropped a half tab of acid an hour before he picked her up,
And didn't say a word until they were driving back & then she said "Blue
    lights . . .
So many blue lights." "Yeah, well, it's the airport. We're driving by the airport
    now,"

He explained. "Oh," she said. Maybe it was the acid that had made her seem

As distant & withdrawn as the world was, stretched across a quiet evening.
Where was *Wild Thing?* Dawn was hazy, overcast, & about as much
Fun to be with as the third wife at the wedding of a Spanish Fork polygamist.

The woman in her hopeless gingham dress had looked on, smiled at her
    husband,
Then at the teenage bride. "You kin to her?" she had asked him. He had come
With a friend who thought the whole thing would be amusing, he had no idea
    who

The girl was. "That little slut?" he had wanted to say because he wanted to say

Something shocking. He still wanted to until the woman turned to him & said,
"With so many people showin' up, we're stretching it pretty thin. But we got
    chili dogs
And ice cream anyway. We splurged." The way someone had carefully trimmed
The yard with its small, parched lawn, & strung balloons on a clothesline
    suddenly
Filled him with pity. Faith showed itself in the rib cage. Its bones were visible.
He could see them beneath the too-small bodice of the woman's dress

Faith resided there, under the shriveled & lost left nipple.

He liked music. He liked hearing it while he worked.

And now he owned the store, although, for an hour or two each night,
He was both blind & mad & believed in kings. And believed he was a king,
And it never once entered his mind that the pencil balanced between

The pulse of his temple & his ear had been invented long after the deaths of
    kings.
After they had done the scene, he would remember who he was again,
An ordinary man who knew it & would have been insane because of knowing it

If he could not crawl toward Dover on his knees. He couldn't act.

When he dressed in weeds, his Temple garment showed under them.
One day he pretended he was a king who had disguised himself as the owner
Of a record store. The king sold eighteen new Donny & Maries before

He abdicated his vinyl throne & went home. If he fell from a high place it would be
A canyon wall he thought he remembered well enough to climb alone.
The water in the stream beneath him would wrinkle & whiten over the rocks as it

Always had & the trees rushing toward him would show him only that they could not

Help it. He knew who he was. Someone would ask him whether he carried
Brahms' *German Requiem,* or Valery Wellington on an extinct Chicago blues label
And he had both. Sometimes he was sick of who he was, & the sickness passed.
The two guys who came in that afternoon were AWOL from a nearby army base,
And maybe only intended to rob the place, & had no idea who they were.
There was a young woman who worked afternoons there & her boyfriend had

Stopped by to tease & flirt with her a little. The two men pretended to browse

Through the stacks of record albums for a while, & then made the owner close
The store & marched them down the steps, & made the woman take off her dress,
And made the boyfriend watch as one, & then the other, raped her there.

What happened after that is blind & smells its way to the sea. They forced
The woman & her boyfriend to swallow some Drano from a can, & then flushed
Their mouths with water & made them swallow. But before they found the leftover can

With the snowy crystals in it, or had thought of using it,

One of them must have noticed the owner with the pencil in his ear, then
the short pine two-by-four. "Has the thought ever entered your mind . . . ?"
One of them said after they had made the man lie on the floor, made him lie on his side

With his ear exposed, with his ear turned up to them, listening to everything,
Wondering how an ear could feel naked when it never had before. Did the
    man really
Believe the two of them would let the others live if he would lie as still as
    possible, as they

Had told him to, & let them do it?

This is usually the moment when the Fool is hanged & the poet disappears
    because
He doesn't know what happens next & a hunger with a mouth as small as
    the eye
Of a sewing needle overruns & darkens the flaxen grasses & the willows &
    the staring
Eyes of ponds, & you know there wasn't any king. There was only a man
    who owned
A record store & who believed two murderers would be kind, & keep their
    promises,
And waited for it to happen, lying there on his side, waiting until they were
    ready to drive

The unbelieving pencil through his ear.

That afternoon after he found it,
The music of a keel scrape still in his ears,

Columbus wrote in a journal: "Walking under the trees there
Was the most beautiful thing

I have ever seen." It's what he left out of it, out
Of the entry, that looks back in recognition.

Did he mean walking there? Did he mean the empty, shaded
Spaces beneath the trees where he rested

After sending his men off to accomplish some task?
To find a waterfall & a China behind it?

Did he mean someone he saw?

But the entire point of the entry, the impossible
Chore he had assigned the men,

Was to be left alone there,

With the sky washed clean above him, with the sun
Burning through all its likenesses

To be what it is, by erasing them.

Ecstasy, in the original sense, meant rapture,
Meant standing outside oneself.

If that is what it was,

If he walked beside himself there on the path that led
To the New World, how long

Can it have lasted, & at what point
Did the sunlight weaken on the path & the men come back,

And with them the hollow sound of the wave chop on the hull
And then the whitecaps appearing

And disappearing, & then maps, riggings, finitude, a crust
Of bread left on a cabin sill, & beyond

The porthole & the wheel the sea shattering the sea
Into air, into the shattered, reforming

Sea & sky again, & then into harbors, wharves,
The ancient walls of cities, moats & courtyards & asylums,

And the sun taking its place again in a stained-glass window
As if someone had decreed it so by law, drawn up

In Latin the exact angle of its light?

And the one who saw the place for the first time

While the wind was unblessing the sails, the boy
In the crow's nest, the thief up there,

Paroled from prison by the queen & expecting
The world to end

In one unending fall of water, who watches carefully,
Who keeps the actual feel of rope

In his hand, holds it there until one day he sees

A twig on a small wave, & then another, then
The soaked black curl of bark, & its

Pale underside, & then the first bird, & then
Another, & another?

And me sitting up there with him, invisible,
Beside him in the rigging,

Thinking that if this is the story
The two of us

Are no more significant to it than whitecaps
Far out at sea,

That paradise would make either one of us
Long for a bar with a good pool table,

A beach town, & a rain without end?

And this kid, fifteen years old,
The first to glimpse the New World? He's not saying

A word about it yet,

He's just sitting here, watching a coastline begin
To take a shape.

Let me move to one side so you can hear his thought
Without me in it anymore:

"First thing I'm gonna do is kill Supedas,
Then I'm gonna chop off his hand & boil it

Until my ring falls off. If you help me, Jesus,
Maybe it could be a little bit your ring, too,

But I'm the one who gets to wear it from now on."   .

And the coastline gradually getting larger
From where I sit, the boy beside me planning

What might be, for all I know, the first murder

In the New World, its wilderness spreading
Over his expressionless face? I'm glad

It's not a story.

It's a list of what I cannot touch:

Some dandelions & black-eyed Susans growing back like innocence
Itself, with its thoughtless style,

Over an abandoned labor camp south of Piedra;

And the oldest trees, in that part of Paris with a name I forget,
Propped up with sticks to keep their limbs from cracking,

And beneath such quiet, a woman with a cane,

And knowing, if I came back, I could not find them again;

And a cat I remember who slept on the burnished mahogany
In the scooped-out beveled place on the counter below

The iron grillwork, the way you had to pass your letter *over* him
As he slept through those warm afternoons

In New Hampshire, the gray fur stirring a little as he inhaled;

The small rural post office growing smaller, then lost, tucked
Into the shoreline of the lake when I looked back;

Country music from a lone radio in an orchard there.
The first frost already on the ground.

And those who slipped out of their names, as if *called*
Out of them, as if they had been waiting

To be called:

Stavros lecturing from his bequeathed chair at the Café Midi,
In the old Tower Theatre District, his unending solo

Above the traffic on Olive, asking if we knew what happened
To the Sibyl at Cumae *after* Ovid had told her story,

After Petronius had swept the grains of sand from it, how,

Granted eternal life, she had forgotten to ask for youth, & so,
As she kept aging, as her body shrank within itself

And the centuries passed, she finally

Became so tiny they had to put her into a jar, at which point
Petronius lost track of her, lost interest in her,

And at which point she began to suffocate

In the jar, suffocate without being able to die, until, finally,
A Phoenician sailor slipped the gray piece of pottery—

Its hue like an overcast sky & revealing even less—

Into his pocket, & sold it on the docks at Piraeus to a shop owner
Who, hearing her gasp, placed her in a birdcage

On a side street just off Onmonios Square, not to possess her,

But to protect her from pedestrians, & the boys of Athens rattled
The bars of her cage with sticks as they ran past yelling,

"Sibyl, Sibyl, what do you want?"—each generation having to
Listen more closely than the one before it to hear

The faintest whispered rasp from the small bitter seed
Of her tongue as she answered them with the same

Remark passing through time, "I want to die!" As time passed & she
Gradually grew invisible, the boys had to press

Their ears against the cage to hear her.

And then one day the voice became too faint, no one could hear it,
And after that they stopped telling

The story. And then it wasn't a story, it was only an empty cage.
That hung outside a shop among the increasing

Noise of traffic, &, from the square itself, blaring from loudspeakers,
The shattered glass & bread of political speeches

That went on half the night, & the intermittent music of strip shows
In summer when the doors of the bars were left open,

And then, Stavros said, the sun shone straight through the cage.

You could see there was nothing inside it, he said, unless you noticed
How one of the little perches swung back & forth, almost

Imperceptibly there, though the street was hot, windless; or unless
You thought you saw a trace of something flicker across

The small mirror above the thimbleful of water, which of course
Shouldn't have been there, which should have evaporated

Like the voice that went on whispering ceaselessly its dry rage

Without listeners. He said that even if anyone heard it,
They could not have recognized the dialect

As anything human.

He would lie awake, the only boy in Athens who

Still heard it repeating its wish to die, & he was not surprised,
He said, when the streets, the bars & strip shows,

Began to fill with German officers, or when the loudspeakers
And the small platform in the square were, one day,

Shattered into a thousand pieces.

As the years passed, as even the sunlight began to seem
As if it was listening to him outside the windows

Of the Midi, he began to lose interest in stories, & to speak
Only in abstractions, to speak only of theories,

Never of things.

Then he began to come in less frequently, & when he did,
He no longer spoke at all. And so,

Along the boulevards in the winter the bare limbs of the trees
One passed in the city became again

Only the bare limbs of trees; no girl stepped into them
To tell us of their stillness. We would hear

Rumors of Stavros following the gypsy Pentecostalists into
Their tents, accounts of him speaking in tongues;

Glossolalia, he once said, which was all speech, & none.

In a way, it didn't matter anymore. Something in time was fading—
And though girls still came to the café to flirt or argue politics

Or buy drugs from the two ancient boys expressionless as lizards
Now as they bent above a chessboard—

By summer the city parks had grown dangerous.

No one went there anymore to drink wine, dance, & listen
To metal amplified until it seemed, as it had

Seemed once, the bitter, cleansing angel released at last from what
Fettered it inside us. And maybe there

Wasn't any angel after all. The times had changed. It became
Difficult to tell for sure. And anyway,

There was a law against it now; a law against gathering at night
In the parks was actually all that the law

Said was forbidden for us to do, but it came to the same thing.
It meant you were no longer permitted to know,

Or to decide for yourself,

Whether there was an angel inside you, or whether there wasn't.

Poverty is what happens at the end of any story, including this one,
When there are too many stories.

When you can believe in all of them, & so believe in none;
When one condition is as good as any other.

The swirl of wood grain in this desk: is it the face of an angel, or
The photograph of a girl, the only widow in her high school,

After she has decided to turn herself

Into a tree? (It was a rainy afternoon, & her van skidded at sixty;
For a split second the trunk of an oak had never seemed

So solemn as it did then, widening before her.)

Or is it misfortune itself, or the little grimace the woman
Makes with her mouth above the cane,

There, then not there, then there again?

Or is it the place where the comparisons, the little comforts
Like the cane she's leaning on, give way beneath us?

What do you do when nothing calls you anymore?
When you turn & there is only the light filling the empty window?

When the angel fasting inside you has grown so thin it flies
Out of you a last time without your

Knowing it, & the water dries up in its thimble, & the one swing
In the cage comes to rest after its almost imperceptible,

Almost endless, swaying?

I'm going to stare at the whorled grain of wood in this desk
I'm bent over until it's infinite,

I'm going to make it talk, I'm going to make it
Confess everything.

I was about to ask you if you were cold, if you wanted a sweater,
Because . . . well, as Stavros would say

Before he began one of those

Stories that seemed endless, the sun pressing against
The windows of the café & glinting off the stalled traffic

Just beyond them, this could take a while;

I pass the letter I wrote to you over the sleeping cat & beyond

   the iron grillwork, into the irretrievable

One was a bay cowhorse from Piedra & the other was a washed-out palomino
And both stood at the rail of the corral & both went on aging
In each effortless tail swish, the flies rising, then congregating again

Around their eyes & muzzles & withers.

Their front teeth were by now yellow as antique piano keys & slanted to the
  angle
Of shingles on the maze of sheds & barn around them; their puckered

Chins were round & black as frostbitten oranges hanging unpicked from
  the limbs
Of trees all through winter like a comment of winter itself on everything
That led to it & found gradually the way out again.

In the slowness of time. Black time to white, & rind to blossom.
Deity is in the details & we are details among other details & we long to be

Teased out of ourselves. And become all of them.

The bay had worms once & had acquired the habit of drinking orange soda
From an uptilted bottle & nibbling cookies from the flat of a hand, & liked
  to do
Nothing else now, & the palomino liked to do nothing but gaze off

At traffic going past on the road beyond vineyards & it would follow each car
With a slight turning of its neck, back & forth, as if it were a thing

Of great interest to him.

If I rode them, the palomino would stumble & wheeze when it broke
Into a trot & would relapse into a walk after a second or two & then stop
Completely & without cause; the bay would keep going though it creaked

Underneath me like a rocking chair of dry, frail wood, & when I knew it could
   no longer
Continue but did so anyway, or when the palomino would stop & then take

Only a step or two when I nudged it forward again, I would slip off either one
   of them,
Riding bareback, & walk them slowly back, letting them pause when they
   wanted to.

At dawn in winter sometimes there would be a pane of black ice covering
The surface of the water trough & they would nudge it with their noses or
   muzzles,
And stare at it as if they were capable of wonder or bewilderment.

They were worthless. They were the motionless dusk & the motionless

Moonlight, & in the moonlight they were other worlds. Worlds uninhabited
And without visitors. Worlds that would cock an ear a moment
When the migrant workers come back at night to the sheds they were housed in

And turn a radio on, but only for a moment before going back to whatever

Wordless & tuneless preoccupation involved them.

The palomino was called Misfit & the bay was named Querido Flacco,
And the names of some of the other shapes had been Rockabye
And Ojo Pendejo & Cue Ball & Back Door Peter & Frenchfry & Sandman

And Rolling Ghost & Anastasia.

Death would come for both of them with its bridle of clear water in hand
And they would not look up from grazing on some patch of dry grass or even

Acknowledge it much; & for a while I began to think that the world

Rested on a limitless ossuary of horses where their bones & skulls stretched
And fused until only the skeleton of one enormous horse underlay
The smoke of cities & the cold branches of trees & the distant

Whine of traffic on the interstate.

If I & by implication therefore anyone looked at them long enough at dusk
Or in moonlight he would know the idea of heaven & of life everlasting
Was so much blown straw or momentary confetti

At the unhappy wedding of a sister.

Heaven was neither the light nor was it the air, & if it took a physical form
It was splintered lumber no one could build anything with.

Heaven was a weight behind the eyes & one would have to stare right through it
Until he saw the air itself, just air, the clarity that took the shackles from his eyes
And the taste of the bit from his mouth & knocked the rider off his back

So he could walk for once in his life.

Or just stand there for a moment before he became something else, some
Flyspeck on the wall of a passing & uninterruptible history whose sounds
      claimed
To be a cheering from bleachers but were actually no more than the noise

Of cars entering the mouth of a tunnel.

And in the years that followed he would watch them in the backstretch or the
      far turn
At Santa Anita or Del Mar. Watch the way they made it all seem effortless,

Watch the way they were explosive & untiring.

And then watch the sun fail him again & slip from the world, & watch
The stands slowly empty. As if all moments came back to this one, inexplicably
To this one out of all he might have chosen—Heaven with ashes in its hair

And filling what were once its eyes—this one with its torn tickets
Littering the aisles & the soft racket the wind made. This one. Which was his.

And if the voice of a broken king were to come in the dusk & whisper
To the world, that grandstand with its thousands of empty seats,

Who among the numberless you have become desires this moment

Which comprehends nothing more than loss & fragility & the fleeing of flesh?
He would have to look up at quickening dark & say: *Me. I do. It's mine.*

There is this sunny place where I imagine him.
A park on a hill whose grass wants to turn
Into dust, & would do so if it weren't
For the rain, & the fact that it is only grass
That keeps the park from flowing downhill past
Its trees & past the slender figures in the statues.
Their stone blends in with the sky when the sky
Is overcast. The stone is a kind of rain,
And half the soldiers trapped inside the stone
Are dead. The others have deserted & run home.
At this time in the morning, half sun, half mist,
There are usually three or four guys sprawled
Alone on benches facing away from one another.
If they're awake, they look as if they haven't slept.
If they're asleep, they look as if they may not wake . . .
I only imagine it as a sunny place. If they're
Awake, they gaze off as if onto a distant landscape,
Not at the warehouses & the freeway the hill overlooks,
Not onto Jefferson Avenue where, later, they'll try
To score a little infinity wrapped up in tinfoil,
Or a flake of heaven tied up in a plastic bag
And small as their lives are now, but at a city
That is not the real city gradually appearing
As the mist evaporates. For in the real city,
One was kicked in the ribs by a night watchman
Until he couldn't move. Another was
A small-time dealer until he lost his nerve
And would then have become a car thief, if only
The car had started. And the last failed to appear,
Not only for a court date, but for life itself.
In these ways, they are like Poe if Poe had lived
Beyond composing anything, & had been kicked to death
And then dismembered in this park, his limbs
Thrown as far away from what was left of him

As they could be thrown. And they are not like Poe.
The three of them stare off at a city that is there
In the distance, where they are loved for no
Clear reason, a city they walk toward when
They are themselves again, a city
That vanishes each morning in the pale light.
Poe would have admired them, & pitied them.
For Poe detested both the real city with its traffic
Crawling over the bridges, & the city that vanishes.

In autumn the rain slants & flesh turns white.
The tents go up again on the edge of town, &,
In the carny's spiel, everyone gets lost,
And Poe, dismembered, becomes no more than the moral
In the story of his life, the cautionary tale
No better than the sideshow where the boy
With sow's hoofs instead of hands, taps the glass—
Some passing entertainment for the masses.
In the carny's spiel, everyone lost comes
Back again. Even Poe comes back to see
Himself, disfigured, in another. That is what
He's doing here, longing to mingle, invisibly,
With the others on the crowded midway as they lick
Their cotton candy, & stare expressionlessly
At one another. He wants to see the woman
Who has fins instead of arms, & the man without
A mouth. He wants to see the boy behind glass
And his own clear reflection in the glass.
The carnival's so close, only a few blocks,
That he can hear the intermittent off-key music
Wheezing faintly out of the merry-go-round . . .
It might as well be music from the moon.
The traffic never lets him cross. The weeks pass,
And then the months, & then the years with their wars
And the marquees going blank above the streets

Because no one comes anymore. And the crowd,
Filing into the little tent, watches suspiciously,
For the crowd believes in nothing now but disbelief.
And therefore, at the intersection of radiance
And death, the intersection of the real city
And the one that vanishes, Poe is pausing
In the midst of traffic, one city inside the other.
The rain slants. The flesh is a white dust.
The cars pass slowly through him, & the boy keeps
Tapping at the glass, unable to tell his story.

Elegy Ending in the Sound of a Skipping Rope

1.

All I have left of that country is this torn scrap
Of engraved lunacy, worth less now

Than it was then, for then it was worth nothing,
Or nothing more than

The dust a wren bathes in,

The fountain dry in the park off the Zeleni Venac,
The needles of the pines dry above it,

The green shutters of the fruitsellers' stands closed
For the afternoon so that in the quiet it seemed

The wren was the only thing moving in the whole city
As it beat its wings against the stone

To rid itself of lice as the dust rose around it.

The sound of its wings, I remember, was like the sound
Of cards being shuffled, as repetitive

And as pointless.

The characters met on faint blue paper.
They were thin as paper then.

They must be starving now.

I don't feel like explaining it,
And now I have to.

To illustrate its money, the State put lovers on the money,

Peasants or factory workers staring off at something
You couldn't see, something beyond them,

Something that wasn't Titograd
They kept looking at it with their faces

Averted, as if they were watching it take place.

In the casinos, these two lovebirds would lie there
Absorbed in it, staring beyond the green felt

Counters of roulette & baccarat tables, beyond the action,
Beyond the men & women in formal attire.

Then someone told me what the money meant,
What they kept looking at:

They were watching the State wither away.

When I tried to imagine it, all I could see
Was a past

Where the ancient goat paths began reappearing,
Crisscrossing a straighter footpath,

Nothing else there except three pedestals lost in moss,

And a man washing a cart horse with soap & tepid
Water, &, at that moment, placing

A plaster of sticky leaves over the sores on the horse's

Withers, the long muscle in the mare's neck rippling
As he does so, as she goes on grazing without the slightest

Interruption, standing there in the shade of an oak
At the exact spot where the Palace of Justice

Finally turned into the mist it had always resembled.
In the moment before it vanished

Flies still buzzed in lopsided circles in the courtroom

And a witness accidentally inhaled one while testifying,
And then *apologized* to the court, apologized

For inhaling a fly, but no one knew what to say,
The room grew suddenly quiet, & then everything disappeared,

And a crowd strolled out of the matinee into a village
That was waiting for them, strolled casually

Out of history,

And into something else: forgetful, inexact,

A thirst, an arousal, a pairing off with whomever they desired,

Strangers even, trysting against walls,

Or in a field of dandelions, on wagonbeds, the moment
Scripted in the involuntary,

Lovely convulsion of thighs lathered as a horse's back,
Because, as Marx said,

Sex should be no more important than a glass of water.

I can't imagine it back.

I can't get the miles of dust rubbed away from it,
Or the layers of sheetrock.

The fruitseller's stand on Lomina Street with its closed
Green shutters was what

Reminded me of Big Sur in 1967,

Reminded me of the beach at Lucia with the vacant
Concession stand, the two unemployables

Entwined like salt in a wave inside it, asleep,
Naked in each other's arms.

I can't imagine it enough.

I can't imagine how to get back to it, with something
In your eye, something always in your eye,

And everything becoming a scrap of paper:

The sprawl of the surf there & the cries of the lovers
Just pin-ups or illustrations behind the counter now:

"Gimme a Coke. Gimme a hot dog too, then," someone
Says to him, tattoos from the navy over

His forearms, not liking what he does, not
Imagining doing anything else now

Except this. Just this.

What withered away?

I watch the guy working fast & suddenly it's *me* who's

Wrapping the hot dogs in waxed paper, *me* who
Half turns, grabs the lids & straws for the Cokes,

Adds it up without pausing & hands them the change.

I can't imagine it enough, & even if I could, one day

That, too, would be the wave's sprawl on the empty rocks,
The hunger in the cries of the gulls.

He pulls the shutters down & locks it up.

"Gimme This & Gimme That. You O.K., Mr. Sea?"
He says to the sky, to the gulls,

To the slur of water receding
On the rocks, to the empty sprawl of the wave

Showing its hand at last before it folds.

2.

The lovers must have stepped out of their money
A few days after the State stepped out

Of its thousand offices.

At night you could look up, & all the black glass
Of the windows would glint back at you

Once, as if in recognition.

The lovers must have stepped out because I *saw* them

Sitting at one of the tables outside the Moskva & shouting
At each other, shouting so loudly

They did not notice their friends beginning
To gather around them.

I gazed past them at the crowds on Terazije passing by
Amid the smells of exhaust

And grilled meat & the odor the sticky bark of the trees
Gave off in the summer afternoon,

The leaves still & exhausted & not turning or
Falling or doing anything yet

Above it all. I liked them. I liked the way the leaves
Had a right to be there & say nothing about it

Hanging there, motionless, without expression,
Without faces, not looking at all

Like passing generations but exactly as leaves look

When they're still, looking as if
They are refusing to enlist, looking as they always did,

If I glanced up from the book I was reading,
And rubbed my eyes,

And tried to trace her shape I had thought
I'd memorized,

But hadn't.

Her shape like the sun on the roads.

Too bad, with all the evacuations,
All the troop movements & closed offices,

Each black window shining like a contradiction,

"You'd think the Parliament would . . .
You would think out of common *decency,* that . . ."

But the State did not wither away,
It looked just the same, with the rain

Falling between the treeless, bleached yellow
Of cheap housing projects, the rain

Showing them the way home, showing them the Future:

When they get there they find her uncle living
With them, he's eating dinner

When they arrive, he's sucking on a fish bone
When they walk in.

In a few weeks Failure & Limitation
Shows its hand in the cold bud

Of her body refusing to open itself,
Refusing to wake up in the morning,

And the uncle by the end of summer walking naked
Through the apartment, pausing one day

Beside her, leaning over her a little, not to
Seduce her but to show her a few things,

To introduce her to

The real head of state grinning through its veil

Of skin as if there was

This joke, something just between

The two of them.
And later the uncle just grins at her,

Grins & says nothing.

Love's an immigrant, it shows itself in its work.
It works for almost nothing.

When the State withers away it resembles
The poor sections of Wichita or Denver.

They held hands the first day & walked under the trees,
And so they were warned about the trees,

About straying into the parks.

A fuzzy haze of green in someone's yard comes back,
But then it forgets it's there.

The streets are forgetting they are streets
And they cross other streets

And at the intersections those streets
Begin to forget.

Most of the stores are boarded up, most of what
Is left is braced with two-by-fours in X's

Over the doors like spells with no power in them,
The sun like neglect bathing the walls,

Bathing the beams you can see right through to,

It's always the day after the day after here,
And every rebellion's a riot,

The riot goes on though no one's there, the streets
Looking burned still, looking as inexplicable

To them as it did the first day
They saw it,

The *days* are inexplicable,
Their unvarying routine where children not yet

In school peer through the chain link
Of a storm fence above the boulevard & the traffic

To watch for cops,

Where their older brothers with their girlfriends
Sprawl on a car seat ripped out

Of a van & placed here to overlook the city, the river,
Its history an insult in which

They were property.

When it was over, history became a withered arm,
And everyone entered history & no one could find them.

The children keep staring through the chain links

Of the storm fence. The older ones on the car seat
Get high from a glass pipe & watch

The planes on the runway taxi & take off,
They get high again & watch the planes

Glide in & land, & do one last hit before
They stand up & one of them pisses into a small ravine

Of trash. The five-year-old girl keeps peering
Through the storm fence without letting

Her attention stray

Because the price of freedom is eternal vigilance,
Her brother tells her, laughing,

And because the task assigned to her is sacred.
I can't imagine her enough.

I remember standing in broken glass at the foot
Of a stairway, the woman beside me

Frightened & crying, & the way the glass felt
Like a river freezing under my feet.

I remember how expensive it all seemed,

And after we had split up, in the years that followed.
I would feel my body turn

Slowly away from others so that it could live alone,
So that each afternoon it could

Become wholly a body. It swept the floors of the house
Each day until it was a routine,

Until it became the finite, thoughtless beauty
Of habit.

Whenever the body swept, it could forget.

And the habit was neither pleasure nor work but an act
That kept the stars above it

In the night, kept the pattern of the stars
From rattling out of their frames,

Whether you could see them above you or not,
Whether you looked up & noticed them or not,

The body swept the floors & kept the light above it.

This is why

The girl keeps squinting through the storm fence,
This is why the task assigned to her is sacred,

Why her love for her brother
Is unconditional,

And though she suspects that her brother
Will one day turn into mist behind her,

A space on the car seat, that he will
Disappear like the others have,

It hasn't happened yet.

I swept the floors to let the worlds blur
Into one another.

But the lovers, the emigrants?
I never see them anymore.

I don't know where they went.

3.

I remember the idiot in the park near Zeleni Venac,
Standing there without a shirt on

With his fly undone,

The way he'd hold his penis in one hand, & simply howl
And keep howling to anyone passing by

On Lomina Street, because, as Ratko explained it to me,
He believed that he held one end of a leash

In his hand, & that the other end was held by his Master,
And now that it had been snapped in two

He would never find him, this Master he had waited for,
This owner whose whistle he listened for

In the faint blue stillness of the summer daybreak.

In the mornings he would seem calm & play cards
Without understanding them with the others

Who slept in the park & tolerated him, but by
Late afternoon he would begin

To stammer & beg beside the dry fountain, the pine needles
So dry by now they seemed

About to ignite above him, & then, at the certain moment,
He would seem to realize

What had happened, he would become completely still
At that moment, & then . . .

Then the howling would start up again.
It was not the howling of an idea.

It was the flesh being flayed.

My friend Ratko used to drink brandy constantly

In little sips throughout the day & could lie
So beautifully about anything

That the government awarded him, each year, a grant

To write stories, but of course he never wrote them
Except on the air as he walked with friends

Through the city.

Continuing his almost endless commentary,
Asking if the idiot did not admit, without knowing it,

The great truth

About us, that a broken string or snipped-off thread
Is all we remember, & that even this is

Less real than the pulpy flesh he held between his fingers.

History has a withered arm.

And the love of these two adhering to paper, delusional,
Vestigial, the daydream of Capitalism,

The last transaction of the State by which it vanishes,

The flies caking the face of the horse standing there
In its innocence again,

I can't imagine them enough to bring them back.
After a while, when any subject is forbidden,

All thought is deviationist.

And the young schoolteacher in Rijeka is . . . *where* by now?
And the young Muslim poet from Sarajevo is . . . *where* by now?

And the harmless lazy bellman at the Atina Palace is . . .
Where by now?

And the pipe-smoking translator with his office overlooking
Princip Street & the river,

Who was last heard on the phone shouting to someone
As the beams & window glass let go of themselves

In the laughter that shatters all things is . . . *where* by now?

Those nights when I couldn't sleep in Belgrade,
When I could no longer read,

When there was no point in going out because everything
Was closed, I'd glance at the two of them

On their worthless currency, as if I might catch them
Doing something else, & once,

I turned from their portrait to the empty street
Beneath the window, the thick trees like a stillness

Itself in the night,
And . . . I *saw* them there. This time they were

Fucking in the rain, their clothes strewn beneath them

On the street like flags

After a war, after some final defeat—fucking each other
While standing up, standing still in the rain & the rain falling

In sheets as if there were no tomorrow left
In it, as if their mouths, each wide open & pressed against

The other's mouth, stilling the other's, & reminding me
Of leaves plastered to the back of a horse

Trotting past after a storm, leaves plastered to the side
Of a house by the wind, to what is left of some face . . .

Had taken the breath out of everything. I thought of
The horse passing easily

Under the exhausted-looking mulberry trees, under the leaves
And the haunted scripture—

Some of its characters shaped like blossoms, others
Like a family of crows taking flight, others like farm tools

Some of them moving in circles like swirls in a current—

All of it written in the cracked, weathered Cyrillic of some
Indecipherable defeat, though once its shapes had been

Perfect for showing one things, clear as a girl's face,

The girl who skipped rope in her communion dress,
          Dry & white as a petal—

          Jedan. Cesto?, Nema, Zar ne?
                    Chaste & thoughtless as the thing she chanted

And then lost interest in, until I could hear only the endless,
Annoying, unvarying flick of the rope each time

It touched the street.

⚘ Afterword

David St. John

It is not an exaggeration to say that the death of Larry Levis in 1996—of a heart attack, at forty-nine—sent a shock wave through the ranks of American poetry. Not only was Levis a good friend to many poets (not simply of his own generation, but of many poets older and younger as well), but his poetry had become a kind of touchstone for many of us, a source of special inspiration and awe. With Larry Levis's death came the sense that an American original had been lost.

A native of California's central San Joaquin Valley, its endless rows of vineyards, its groves of fig and almond orchards, Larry Levis brought to his poetry John Steinbeck's dramatic sweep of the landscape. Although Levis came of age in the late sixties, it was his upbringing on his family farm that helped to provide the sense of social conscience that resonates in all of his work. It was a time when César Chávez brought the plight of farmworkers to the world stage; but for Levis those questions always remained personal and intimate, the stories of particular young men whose voices spoke alongside him in the fields of his childhood.

I should hasten to add that Larry Levis was a highly worldly and urbane poet as well. In the six books of poetry from which this collection is drawn, Levis had charted a course that itself reads somewhat like a précis of poetic endeavor in American poetry since the mid-sixties. His early work—the first three collections were all prize-winning volumes—moves from a deep-image lyricism to a more highly reflective and meditative mode. His mature poetry, as embodied by the two remarkable books *Winter Stars* and *The Widening Spell of the Leaves,* as well as the posthumously published collection, *Elegy,* exhibits an even more relaxed, discursive, and wry philosophical style.

Levis's final poetry often reveals the harsh nature of poetry as our age has insisted upon it, carrying Levis's speculative impulse far into the mind's shadows; these poems are often fragrant with death. His meditations lift us into realms—some real, some imagined—that grow increasingly harrowing. The echoes of lost voices resound everywhere in his mature poems as they gather into fables and narratives of the century's collapse. If such a thing is possible, Levis's late poems seem poignantly apocalyptic, moving, as he says in *Elegy,* "toward the blank / Sail of the sky at the end of the world." Yet for Levis, "Death" is never the stern Reaper; he is instead the cosmically bored magician, the oily sleight-of-hand man at some county fair. Death is just another indignation to endure, the supreme banality.

Throughout his career, Larry Levis's poems remained gracefully conversational. Levis trusts always in the pleasure of language, the pleasures of thought. His sentences unravel slowly, twisting and rippling, gathering in force and definition. His poems are filled with a rugged grandeur, the inspired gestural sprawl of a Whitman-gone-West; they reflect his desire for a conversation with the world at large, and many of Levis's poems turn to the natural world as an imperfect but necessary mirror.

To have a true sense of Larry Levis's poems, especially his mature work, one must try to imagine Rilke's great "Duino Elegies" spoken not from the parapets of high Romanticism but from a dusty, heat-baked grape field in Levis's native Selma, California. Remarkably, Levis manages to wear his wisdom like a shrug, not like a prophet's mantle. Clearly, Levis envisions many of his poems as a kind of self-deliverance from the convention of death as an ending, death as a nightmare. He believes in the simple dignity of human beings, and what we constantly discover in these poems is Levis's hope in a desperate tenderness that might rescue us from our notions of oblivion.

This often-compromised hope and Levis's faith in the transforming ability of the imagination remain the deep subjects of his poetry. Where other poets might turn to proclamation, Levis grows playful, ironic, and at times hilariously absurd. Levis can capture the dark declarative deadpan of a writer like Milan Kundera only to riddle and interrupt the surface of his poems with moments reminiscent of Gabriel Garcia Marquez.

Often, Levis's championing of those at the margins of society—migrant workers, the dispossessed, a variety of spiritual transients—is set against a landscape of encroaching mortality. Nevertheless, he is fated to live without the fierce optimism finally necessary to rescue his figures from their destinies, and in the end it sometimes seems only the act of poetry itself that holds Levis from the edge of a true despair.

The progress of Larry Levis's final three collections—*Winter Stars, The Widening Spell of the Leaves,* and the posthumous volume, *Elegy*—reflects a complex midlife reckoning with death's allure and power, its intrusions upon the desires and hopes of the living. One of the profound ironies of these poems is that Levis takes as his project the befriending of death, in order to honor— yet to reconcile and neutralize—the drama of its power, its grip on our consciousness. It is sometimes the ease of the befriending in these poems that feels especially disturbing and prescient.

Since the book *Winter Stars,* Larry Levis has been asking how can we *not* collapse under the weight of our responses to a world so replete with horrors. He has also asked us to examine and condemn our own growing numbness to that world. It is not at all paradoxical that he saw both the most intimate expressions of poetry and the grandest gestures of art, of language, as constituting individual acts of courage. One can only hope that, like such courage, Larry Levis's remarkable poems will continue to live far into our literature.

The Selected Levis was designed and typeset in Minion with Arial Black display type by Kachergis Book Design, Pittsboro, North Carolina.